FROM indicating the point in space at which a journey, motion, or action starts. indicating a source of knowledge or the basis for one's judgement.

BITTER feeling or showing anger, hurt, or resentment because of bad experiences or a sense of unjust treatment.

TO expressing motion in the direction of. used to introduce the second element in a comparison.

BETTER more desirable, satisfactory, or effective. improve on or surpass (an existing or previous level or achievement).

Copyright © 2019 by April Broomhead

All rights reserved. This book or any portion thereof may not be reproduced or used in any manner whatsoever without the express written permission of the publisher except for the use of brief quotations in a book review. Sale of this book without its official uncover is unauthorised. For permission requests write to the publisher at beingmeinthisworld@gmail.com

The information in this book is for guide and reference only and is not to substitute a medical practitioner. The author of this book does not dispense medical advice nor prescribe the use of any technique as a form of treatment for physical or medical problems without the advice of a physician either directly or indirectly. The intent of the author is only to offer information of a general nature to support your journey to full health, mind body and spirit.

The author and the publisher assume no responsibility for your actions.

First Printing, 2019

Self-Published By Ingram Spark

ISBN: 978-0-473-50158-7

www.consciousfamilydynamics.com
instagram: @iamaprilbroomhead
email: beingmeinthisworld@gmail.com

"Time Wont Heal A Thing. It Is What You Choose To Do With That Time, That Does"

"Well, What Are You Waiting For? Lets Begin!"

Intention

It is simple, my intention is to guide you through the dark night of the soul, into your natural state of parenting so that you can be deeply connected to your tamariki, by supporting you whilst you let go of the ways that do not serve your evolving, and create new ways of being.

APRIL BROOMHEAD

Dedication

This book is dedicated to the girl in the mirror alongside with my ancestors and Mama Earth, tangata whenua. Thank you for never leaving me and for walking me home to myself and my roots.

To my born to parents who can at times be triggered by the words I share. I chose you. I don't know how I am the way I am, with this feeling inside me that has always been here, we can blame in on Granny if you like. I am happy. Thank you for not trying to tame me. We will be who we are meant to be, irrespective of our parents, if only we are allowed space to be who we are. You both gave me that.

To my other mums, Genine you taught me emotions and nurture. You taught me how to manage a home, hang the washing properly and cook mean roast potatoes. I have never once looked at you and thought you were not capable; you are probably one of the most capable people I have ever known. Never underestimate the power of what cooked porridge and moving firewood can do for a person's tenacity in life. You are directly responsible for my lifelong thirst to have initiative.

Louise, you taught me to walk with in faith and rise above the flesh. You taught me how lying on the couch crying and being putu was not a failure, it was a time for nurture. You taught me about nurture and asking for support. You have without a doubt been walking this path with me and I do hope that you bring to life your intuitive creations. I made a promise to Addison before she was born, and that was that no matter my relationship with my mother in law, she would always be allowed a choice in who she relates to. There is no such thing as "just a mum". You are directly responsible for me understanding the words

"I Need You To Be Brave Now, Be Courageous"

greetings

PART: WELCOME

"Come On In"

"Only A Man Who

is constantly seeking betterment of his self will be allowed to leave his slippers under my bed"

The Calling

Come on in, welcome to our space. Together with you and the universe, I have been cultivating our space. Infusing it with magic. Loading it with the feels and the safety you will need to surrender into this transformation.

This book is not for the average gal. She is not going to end up with the masses. This piece of magic is for the front-line woman. The woman I see when I do my intuitive drawings. Close your eyes. Tell me, can you see the tribe?

"I Am Calling For You To Step Up. Hear My CALL, Take The Step. It Is Time"

Children feel everything and at some stage you may have to accept that families don't need to live together to be a family. We are most powerful as parents when we stand in our own confidence.

Choose to live on purpose and show your children how to get back up when life knocks them down. The longer you stay out of alignment to your true purpose, the more your soul dies.

This is the rising and returning of the parents.

"You Did Not Seek This Book, This Book Sought You"

Dear All The Mums

"It Wasn't Supposed To Be Easy, It Was Meant To Be Natural"

Dear Mums,

Our people once were warriors. These words are for you.

To all the mum's who have ever stood in the school and cried coz, well, fuck! The mums who have whisper screamed "put your shoes on now!" To the mums who have passively let their possessed child stay up past midnight because "ain't no one got time for that."

The mums who have wanted to step to a school ground biarch, because of the way they made their child cry. The mums who rock up to school in their pajamas and kick the kids out before going home to cry. The mums who can't wait for the kids to go to sleep and then misses them.

And these mums; The mums who walked away from their children, because it was that or jump off a bridge.

The woman who loved/love men who already have children. Bam you're a step mum now. Forever to be reminded that you are not Mum.

The woman who are watching other woman raise their child with jealousy and fear. Scorned at the wrench who broke their marriage trying to find a way to be ok with life as it is. The woman loving and working in the youth system playing mum.

"Without Woman Life Would Cease. Without Men, Life Would Cease"

Bringing life onto this planet, it's not easy. It's not pretty, and it certainly isn't logical. I mean, you think it's about your vagina and then the contractions start, talk about intense!

The path to pregnancy is unique for us all. For some it's a wham bam thank you dam I'm pregnant. For others it's crying on the toilet at another period.

The new couple living in state housing on their 5th child, it's a beautiful first try success whilst the neighbor is on her fourth miscarriage after 4 rounds of ivf, curled up in fetal position on the bathroom floor, stomach cramping, blood, tears, a blackening heart and a failing marriage.

The 40-year-old who despises her husband is secretly at the abortion clinic whilst the successful corporate lady who doesn't want kids is having another conversation about why this choice doesn't make her less a woman.

Then there is the girl who got raped and couldn't tell her parents so ran away and left the baby in a trash can only to feel ashamed every single day. The quiet pill taking to poof, make it go away.

This is my message to you: **Stop judging each other's parenting. You are either helping or getting in the way!**

This day let us together honor every woman. Look around at the woman, relate to her. She has pain just like yours you cannot deny it. She is doing her best.

It takes a world to make a world. Fertility, pregnancy, loss, stillborn, babies, toddlers, preschoolers, teenagers, adults… It's all part of motherhood, it's all part of the womb. The ultimate creation of human life on earth!

For the woman today who is holding it together, ask for what it is you need!

My wish is for people to stop judging and gossiping about mums and how they raise or neglect their children. Leave them the fuck alone or do something to change the culture. No one wakes up and decides to be a shit cunt of a mum. Sorry, but it's the damn truth. We have a lot of work to do here in Aotearoa to break generational wounds and patterns and 1 thing I know to be fact, relentless judgement and condescending looks does not do that.

I have sat with woman who had their children taken from them and are now doing the work. They are in pain. They were raped by uncles and cousins, they were beaten, they lived a once were fucking warriors upbringing. It is not their fault. It was the hand they were dealt. So, if you have a better hand, do your part to change our nation.

Our children must be the priority. Everything you do whilst they are little is so that you can raise them better. Domestic violence in New Zealand is shocking. It breaks my heart; I'm literally crying at star bucks right now. I had no intention of sharing these feels with you, but the book has a hold on me.

No child is a bad child. There are some, that you must keep your child away from, that does not make that child a bad child. Our jobs as parents is to protect our children. Know when to allow them a lesson and when to keep them safe. You do not know strength until you must stand for your child against someone you love.

"You Must Choose Your Child. They Have Nothing If They Do Not Have You"

If it is too late, and something has already happened with your child's innocence, get coaching for you. People often seek support for the children, yet they don't have support for themselves. This is why I coach parents; I coach parents to stand for the children by standing for themselves. If you are in the hole with the child, you are of no help. Get out.

I speak with woman everyday who are hurting, triggered in anxiety because of the judgements of others, especially family. Offer support or fuck off.

My people ask for what you need. It isn't chocolate. There are hundreds of people working to support mums in rising and returning.

I love flowers I really do, but man, we need more than pretty flowers in a vase to raise our children better.

The Woman

A beautiful sensual woman is standing in the forest, alone and naked, her hair blowing softly in the breeze.

She starts to run through the trees, the freshly fallen snow unrelenting beneath her tired feet.

She feels lost.

She is searching for her child.

She falls to the ground surrendering to her maker, her hot burning tears the only reminder that she is still alive.

The dark night swoops in and begins to take her soul.

"To Meet The Woman, You Must Meet The Girl"

The Girl

Inside an antique cream mirror is a gorgeous, little girl.

To the naked eye she would appear to be about 5 years old, her eyes are kind, her hair is soft and shiny, and her complexion is innocent.

You notice something about her, something that makes you want to stop and ask her what she is doing inside this mirror.

Waiting, she tells you in a birdlike voice.

Her face is strikingly pretty and warm.

You ask her what she is waiting for and with her eyes, the same sort of eyes you would see in a child waiting at school for a parent who had forgotten about her, she answers you.

She longs for someone to notice her, to listen to her, hold her and show her she matters.

She is waiting for love and acceptance.

She has so many ideas to share about how to make life wonderful, and, she tells you, she holds the secrets to your life purpose.

You feel weirdly compelled to her, it's almost like you know her.

"We Are All Longing For Intimacy & Safety"

In The Mirror

You don't have to be that lost woman in the woods anymore.

When did you stop listening to the little girl inside you?

When did you leave her alone in the mirror?

The big question people ask themselves is, should I stay, or should I go. I'm here to tell you that there are better questions.

Once you realise that the answers all lie within your, change will happen.

I would like you to begin to look in the mirror every day, ask yourself who is this girl that stands before you in the mirror.

> How can I know that I am good enough?
> How can I keep my word to myself?
> How can I choose the girl in the mirror?

"You Can Never Escape Yourself, May As Well Get To Like Yourself"

Aotearoa Needs Us

"I Am The Motherland And The Motherland Is Me"

An uber driver told me that he scoffs at millennials who live in their mother's basement and preach about saving the earth. He said they have no idea and should get a real job, try a long-term relationship, be a parent. You know, all the things normal responsible adults do.

Inside my mind I thought, well dude, if there is no earth there are no jobs, no marriage, no children… nothing to be responsible for.

I'm trying this new thing where I don't make anyone wrong, so I did not voice my opinions. I agree with the perspective and then offer a small nugget of my perspective instead and leave them to it.

The thing is there is a gap. Conflicts, lots of raging at people to care about the things they don't have the capacity to care about. What I feel we need, is to meet in the middle.

I care about the earth mainly because I am a mum, and an aunty. I can't not care now. Who am I kidding, I feel the land, I am after all, a native.

"I Brought Life Onto This Planet So Earth Is My Responsibility"

Another perspective I have is this. What's the point of saving the earth if we continue to raise paedophiles, woman beaters, corrupt politicians, home wreckers, narcissists and allow homeless people to be less important than street art.

90% of my focus goes on being a better mum. That includes caring about the earth. Included in that is "how can I serve the world with the gifts I naturally have."

I'm not going to always donate to the earth causes. I'm not going to always recycle. I'm not always going to use natural cleaning products or share on my social media the worlds issue. I am not the news. I do not have to care about everything.

I have committed to progressively changing to support the earth a little bit every day. Just as I commit to be a bit better at parenting every day.

Everything that we as a collective do to better our planet including the people and or the environment, by default works to save the environment and the people.

Do you get it?

You have a natural gift inside you.

Be your gift, that is the best thing you can do, to save our earth.

"Find Your Purpose, Be Kinder, Act Consciously"

"I Wasn't Searching For The Truth; I Was Searching For The Ability To Handle It"

How I Got Into The Woods

"Get In The Forest And Start Slaying Yo Beasts"

Do you realise that I was that woman that was searching for the mirror? Do you see, that, that was also me?

My soul was dying, I had submitted to the dark, it had moved in on my soul and I was being eaten alive.

When I found myself in the woods, it was cold dark, and the beasts were everywhere waiting to feast on my dead body. I felt exposed and scared for my life, even though I did not want the life.

The reason I was in the woods was because I was looking for the fresh air. I was asking mama earth to come and save me. I told her, take me hard and take me fast. I don't care what it takes, I promise to stay alive. (Be careful what you wish for, you just might get it.)

I was running away from the concrete jungle life. Who was this woman who would go to work and be faced with servings from the tax department, banks trying to repossess the house, employees not showing up because of addictions, family members accused of murder, another trying to extort money for drugs, a cousin committing suicide, a husband who wasn't coming home.

I was seeking a way home. I asked for the path to be shown to me and I was absolutely not ready for it. I was so heavy with mum guilt. I was not showing up empathetically or naturally with my daughter

I was fucking miserable. I was treating people like shit because inside my chest felt so stretched it was about to shatter and I was in pain. So much pain.

I had no idea how to get through it. I went from not ever wanting sex to not being able to get enough of it. I didn't want cuddles, I couldn't damn breath and really, I didn't want anything except to go to sleep and stay asleep.

I quit showing up places because I felt like a fraud. Like does anyone know what a damn lie I'm living! All these people think I live a flashy easy life with a beautiful family. If only they knew.

I believed that most the world hated me. Thought I was scum. Not worthy of anything. And my hormones, I was so close to getting the insides of my uterus burnt so that I could stop suffering PMS. It was torture. Life was torture, I could feel the beasts with their claws in me, I could feel the fangs biting through my chest, I could feel them sucking my life away.

I sometimes feel bad for my then husband, he just couldn't help me. He couldn't support me; he did not know how I had to rise up against my beasts. He didn't know my path. That was not his to know, it is my journey. He needed to find his path and slay his own beasts.

"I Didn't Like Me, I Didn't Want Me"

Of course, over the next 1 to 2 years I played out my childhood story of abandonment and our marriage started to separate when Addison was 6. She was the same age I was when my parents split.

And boy did I break down. And cry. Every day for around 6 hours a day for 6 weeks. I was a wreck when I first learnt how to surrender and stop straining to fix everything. I went on to cry every day for about 10 months, and most days for about 18 months.

I made the ending of my marriage mean that I was the most undesirable female on the planet, I was un-fuckable like the ugly duckling. I hated my walk, my voice, my face, yep, my everything.

I kept thinking I don't deserve this. This isn't fair. I want my life back. I can fix this. Why would he do this to me, to us? How could he do this? And round and round it would go. I was deep in devastation, also known as, Winter.

"Stop Feeding The Beasts April, Get Up"

Before We Go on,

A Couple Of Thank You's

For My Addison Ava

"I Am Capable. I Am Loved."

Did you know that Ava means, like a bird? I added this into your name so that you could never be caged. So that you would know that you had wings in your own very name.

I negotiated with the sky for 4 years before I became with child. I made a promise to the tiny heart & lungs growing inside my womb, to my unborn baby, our Addison, to you.

I promised that "I" would raise you. I would bake you cookies and teach you how to be kind and happy. I promised that I would be happy.

I swore to god I would appreciate you without turning you into a spoilt brat, I would be the mum that you need.

Addison, you will never understand the depth of love that I feel for you. You are the person who truly inspires me.

I adore you. Your ability to let go and carry on, your trust in me, your unconditional love, your style, your smile.

You have shown me how to be me, by being you. I honor you, I am privileged you chose me to be your guide, earth side.

Thank you for your patience and kindness, your sassiness and honestly.

"You My Dear, Are My Legacy, Together We Will Create New Worlds"

ww.consciousfamilydynamics.com

"Love does not

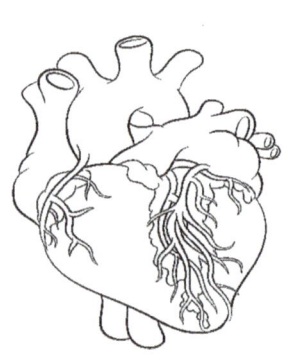 hurt. Anything that hurts is attached to your mind not your heart"

For My Baby Daddy

"The Never-Ending Story"

We often ask for it all, but we usually mean only the good stuff. Curtis, thank you for it all. We had it all. The highs and the lows.

Our ever-changing relationship is without a doubt the biggest facilitation to my growth. I met you as a scared weak angry girl desperately seeking love and acceptance. And you gave me 16 years, a house, a marriage, a business or 3, funerals, friendship, 2 pregnancies and coming up, a divorce.

Thank you for loving our girl, and for correcting me every time I say 'my' girl.

Whatever you may do with your life, your love for our daughter is what makes you a man to me. You are a great dad; I'd never call you good because good only gets you average.

Many men choose to leave, choose to put a barrier around their heart because the pain is too great. They move onto making a new family and forget the heart of the firstborn.

I held faith that your love for her soul would keep you evolving during the times I moved to spaces you could not enter. Spaces that my soul needed me to enter.

Thank you for not giving into the dark night. I know it was excruciating. Thank you for not listening to the projections and pain of people who did not have our Addi at heart.

Whatever contract we signed, up above, in our mad desire for growth, thank you for honoring it. Over and out. OG.

"Greenish Brownish Female Sheep Bro"

For My Sensei

"It Works, If You Work"

I love waking up in the morning, even when it's cold and dark outside.

When Lou told me, she had a life coach I quietly scoffed, pffft that shit does not work. Little did I know, I was going to need a way shower to get me through the woods and the big man up above had decided you would be it. The one requirement, it won't work, if I don't work.

February 2018 I had hit the bottom of my 3rd rock-bottom & I was praying "Scottie beam me up, run me over by a truck, let me have a heart attack just seriously, get me the fuck out of the shit show, this isn't funny anymore!"

Only Scottie didn't beam me up, he connected me to you instead. Not what I was asking for, but fuck it, I had nothing to lose.

"If I go into this space with you April, will you do the work?" "What the fuck is 'space?'" I asked followed up with a, "Yes, but you need to know that I am really difficult."

About 72 hours earlier I had been wailing "I can't do this" whilst whacking my steering wheel, blinded by pain, relentless tears, sweat dripping off every inch of my body.

"I Desperately Wanted To Tap Out"

My head was in excruciating turmoil, my heart felt like it was going to explode and spatter on the windscreen and my throat was aching and terrified at the reality of how much shit I was in.

To say I was broken is an understatement. Life had defeated me. Stab me in the eye with a needle, I wouldn't have felt it.

On our 3rd conversation I told you Emile, that I was 50 shades of fucked up, in response you laughed, a laugh that made me feel like maybe, just maybe, I was not crazy. And just like that I remembered I knew how to make people laugh; I remembered a little bit of the fun bubbly girl I used to be.

"I Won't Be The Waffle Girl"

Emile, you let me feel, like *really* feel. You made it safe for me to show up. You taught me how to let the answers come. You encouraged me to trust myself and reminded me over and over, this too shall pass.

You showed me how to be honest with myself, leaning in when you knew I needed the push and softening back when you knew I needed compassion and time. You knew when I was going to run and you made it easy for me to bench myself instead.

"You Guided Me To My Girl In The Mirror"

You guided me into addressing my anger and hatred, resentments & jealousy, all my mamae. You showed me that sadness was a beautiful emotion to sit with.

You encouraged me to look at the true power of being an empath, told people I was powerful, told me that I was a leader, 'one of us." You watched my process and all my messiness and all the way, you accepted me and told me, "You are not difficult, you're actually really easy."

You made me chicken soup, refused to tell me what to do, brought me lemon water, made fun of my resting bitch face and laughed with me not at me. You constantly reminded me that my best outcome was possible, when all I could see was pain, destruction, fire and waffles.

You told me "April, you are one of the Good ones. The world needs more April Broomheads.'" Steenveld, Emile, I absolutely adore you. Thank you for being with me through my darkest of hours, I would not have carried on if you had not offered me your hand.

Table of Contents

greetings 9

   PART: WELCOME 9

      The Calling 11

      How I Got Into The Woods 22

essence 38

   PART: HEART TRUTH 38

      Set Your Compass 44

      Set The Bullseye 49

      This Ideal Mum 52

      Co-Parenting Dream 54

heartsong 63

   BEING ME 63

      Vibrational Chart 70

      Emotion V's Feeling 86

winter 116

   PART: GOING IN 116

      Winter Needs Nurture 118

      Boundaries 124

      Be Assertive 128

      Making Stories Up 135

autumn 171

   PART: BREATHE OUT 171

      True Colors In Autumn 173

      Letting Go vs Purging 175

      Journaling - Take Two 177

spring 201

PART: BREATHE IN 201
Create & Connect 203
Intuitive Creation 205
I Am In My Own Energy 207

summer 226

PART: UNCONDITIONAL 226
Empowered Action 228

learners 236

PART: EMBODY 236
The Children Are The Future 238
Empathetic Parenting In Action 244
Co-operative Parenting 253
Perfect Parenting 267
Be Courageous, Slay The Beasts 274
Nature Elements 280

seasoned 292

PART: FOUND 292

How To Be Guided

"Overthinking Has Its Perks, Find Them"

You will allow yourself the possibility of a new way, right? Your ways have led you to this point right here, the crossroads. They alone won't be able to get you to the valley of happiness. You will need to pick up some new ways.

The way it works is, I as the coach say something, you try it on for size.

Turn all your focus inwards. Walk towards yourself and banish the word selfish. What is selfish, is walking around in pain and taking it out on others.

This book is set out in parts which I have related to the seasons. Nature plays a huge role in healing and transformation and can teach us a lot about how to view our emotions in a healthy way. We need winter as much as we need summer. We need the night and we need the day. Have you noticed how faithful the sun is, she always rises.

"The Light Is Always There, Just Look For It"

Flowers would not be appreciated if they bloomed all year. Spring would lose its serenity if the winter season was not cold.

For each season imagine a path and picture you on it. Set the scene of your path. Where is it, what do the trees look like? Is there water? Imagine I am there with you.

Imagine that every time you refuse to answer or say, "I don't know", we will need to sit on the path until you do find the answer. If you are in the winter, we stay out in the cold with the beasts hissing from the trees. Turn towards the beasts, you are not afraid. Slay them.

Without the new awareness, we simply cannot connect the dots and get out of the maze. You, you are the only one with the map out of here.

It Is Your Move

At the moment there will be something you do to 'get rid' of the feelings when they arise. It could be so many things such as: drugs, fucking, cooking, cleaning, weights, eating, texting, fussing with kids, working or getting into bed to cry.

What I would like you to do is notice when you have a feeling and then let yourself be guided to a section in the book and fill out a page.

You will have to allow yourself to really answer the questions deeply and let emotions arise and learn how to be with them. Do the work, the tasks. Make the time.

"Keep Your Eye On The Prize, And The Prize Is You"

You will soon learn to identify how you are feeling, with a season, this will just allow you to understand better your process and connect more with nature, our powerful earth mama.

Trust yourself, this is your process.

"Kia Kaha, Kia Maia, Kia Manawanui - Be Strong, Be Brave, Be Steadfast"

No Wrong Way, Just Better

If you have just started your journey, start with winter.

If you feel that you are doing well but still felt compelled to use this book, start in autumn. You won't spend too much time in summer, as summer has the least amount of growth. This book is all about the growth.

It may at times feel like you are going backwards, remember feelings are not facts. Notice how each time you trip and fall, you rise more confidently and with more appreciation for yourself. That is progress.

Please give up negativity including researching through why all men cheat, how horrible narcissism is and why mistresses should all burn in hell. Remove yourself from gossip, learn how to consciously complain, detox from social media. Do not communicate or play games with any mistress or 'other woman."

Forgive yourself if you slip remembering that this takes time. My etheric healer, Crystal Lee, told me once "Even arseholes have a light."

People in pain do terrible horrible things to each other, rise above.

Come back to the path you imagined earlier in this book. How can you shift your energy?

Oh, and, if you are in an abusive relationship, I need you to seek support. You are somewhat blinded to the damage it is doing. You need your energy for your beasts, not his.

"Healing Feels Messy, Yet The Reality Is, The Mess Was Already There"

Intentions Are Destinations

An intention is like telling your brain what to aim for. It's a programming. Set an intention so you can focus on what you are trying to achieve.

→ My intention for using this book is:

Support Leads To Success

"Take The Hand That Is Offered To You"

You may need to consider getting further support. These are some clues that you have a deeper journey ahead of you and would benefit from my private coaching.

You Often Feel Overwhelmed

You feel that you are stuck and are unsure about what you want, what to do, how to do it and where to even begin.

You Hide Your Mess

You show people a perfect home and exterior, but inside you are having panic attacks, depressed feelings and secretly judge people.

You Yell Or Ignore Your Children

You lack the confidence to say yes or no with ease, resulting in extreme behavior's either passive or aggressive, which usually the children cop.

You Can Not Stop The Thinking That Leads You To Panic

You know your thinking takes you down the rabbit hole, yet you do not know how to stop it. Your nights are sleepless, and you feel unorganized.

You Do Not Confide In Anyone

You are too scared to say out loud what is happening. The whole truth scares you.

"When We Are Supported, We Feel Safe To Look Within For Answers, Accept Who We Are And Have Strength & Resilience To Change Our Lives"

"You Didn't See It Coming Because You Eyes Have Been Shut"

essence

PART: HEART TRUTH
"All Of Me"

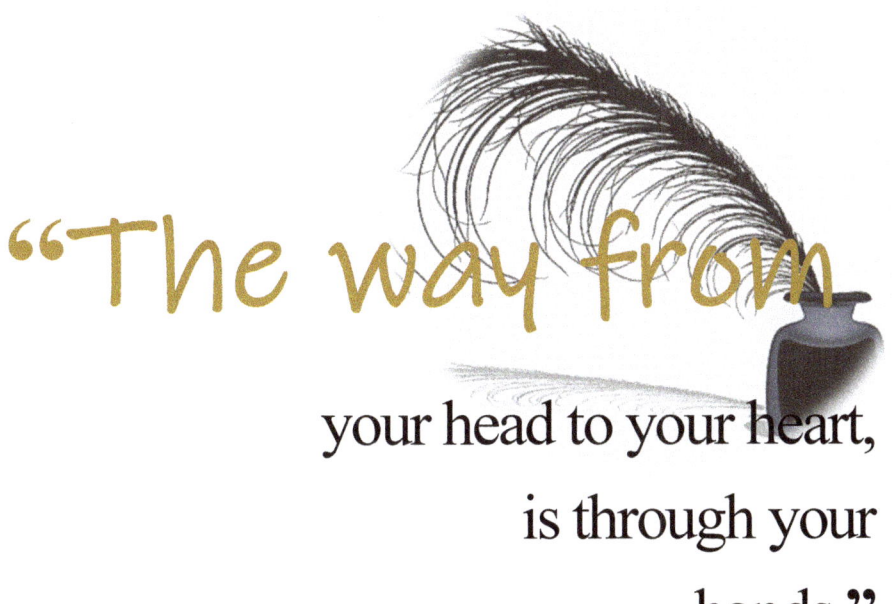

"The way from your head to your heart, is through your hands."

You Are Part Of The Puzzle

"Who Are You, Where Are You & When Are You You"

You would by now be noticing what drains you, the heavy work. What about the light work?

➜ **What gives you energy?**

Right now, you sit in 1 of 3 categories.

> 1 – I am working my life's purpose
> 2 – My purpose is calling me.
> 3 – I have no freaking idea what it is.

For the 1's: - If you are truly already working in your life's purpose, it would surprise me that I am your guide. I am a way shower; people gravitate to me to guide them to their light. I would encourage you to really investigate this section, and ask yourself this;

➜ **What Dream Have I Given Up On?**

For the 2's: - You on a track baby girl. Yeww! This is your sign! This does not mean it will be easier for you, it means that you get to go deeper into actioning the work. Every day ask yourself;

➜ **How Can I Action My Purpose On A Daily Basis?**

For the 3's – When our life purpose is calling us and needs us now, we very often push it down and deny it due to sub-conscious fears. Let all the little things that pop up, pop up and do not place expectations on what it should look like. Before you go to sleep at night, I want you to ask this question;

➜ **How Can I Serve My Purpose?**

→ *I feel comfortable when I am:*

→ *If I had the confidence I would:*

→ *I've always wanted to:*

→ *When I was young, I spent my free time:*

→ *I also loved to:*

Meet Your Future Self

A Visualisation Exercise

→ *Read this paragraph and then action this visualisation.*

Close your eyes and imagine that you are walking up to the door of your home in 10 years' time. What does the house **feel** like, **look** life? Who lives there? What does she smell like, dress like? How does she move? What is her voice like? How do you feel around her?

→ *My future self:*

→ *The lessons and messages she asked me to record are these:*

→ *So that I can embody those lessons, I am now going to let go of:*

→ *I can surrender by:*

→ *I am creating:*

Set Your Compass

"What Do You Stand For My Dear?

→ *Read this paragraph and then do the values exercise on the next page.*

Go deep into your values, values assist you with where you are going in life, who you wish to be around and what to say yes and no to. The saying 'alignment' is based around being aligned with your values. If you don't know them, it is very hit and miss.

"Do not underestimate them"

With your values, I want you to write them out, pretty them up and place them around your house to serve as a visual reminder for you. Every noticed how children have visuals around the school to help them learn? Same for you.

Do not get attached to the words, allow them to change if they do not fit. Know what they mean to YOU, not others.

Most importantly, learn how to live into them by focus on them every day. Pick the value that is least being honored and focus on how you can top it up each day/week by creating daily habits or activities around them.

Values are key to alignment and are worth the effort. Do not be discouraged if you take a while to find yours. I do offer 1 off sessions for discovering values, feel free to contact me. Just mention my book and I'll be sure to prioritise you.

"If You Don't Know What You Stand For, You Will Fall"

Values

What Matters The Most To You?

→ *Circle all the words that describe what matters most to you.*

Abundance	Belonging	Consciousness	Children	Extravagance	Calmness
Acceptance	Benevolence	Consistency	Directness	Extroversion	Camaraderie
Accomplished	Bliss	Contentment	Discipline	Exuberance	Candour
Accuracy	Boldness	Continuity	Discovery	Fairness	Capability
Achievement	Bravery	Contribution	Discretion	Faith	Care
Acknowledgement	Brilliance	Control	Diversity	Family	Celebrity
Activeness	Closeness	Conviction	Expediency	Fascination	Certainty
Adaptability	Comfort	Cooperation	Exploration	Fashion	Challenge
Adoration	Commitment	Correctness	Expressiveness	Fearlessness	Charity
Adventure	Compassion	Courage	Sacredness	Ferocity	Charm
Affection	Completion	Courtesy	Sacrifice	Fidelity	Chastity
Affluence	Composure	Craftiness	Sagacity	Fierceness	Cheerful
Aggressiveness	Concentration	Creativity	Saintliness	Financial	Clarity
Agility	Confidence	Credibility	Sanguinity	Firmness	Cleanliness
Alertness	Conformity	Cunning	Satisfaction	Fitness	Clear minded
Altruism	Congruency	Curiosity	Security	Flexibility	Cleverness
Ambition	Connection	Daring	Seductive	Flow	Dominance
Anticipation	Leadership	Decisiveness	Self-control	Fluency	Dreaming
Appreciation	Learning	Decorum	Selfless	Focus	Drive
Approachability	Liberation	Deference	Self-reliant	Fortitude	Duty
Articulacy	Liberty	Delight	Sensitive	Frankness	Dynamism
Assertiveness	Liveliness	Dependability	Sensual	Freedom	Eagerness
Assurance	Logic	Depth	Serenity	Friendliness	Economy
Attentiveness	Longevity	Desire	Service	Frugality	Ecstasy
Attractiveness	Love	Determination	Sexy	Fun	Education
Audacity	Majesty	Devotion	Sharing	Gallantry	Effectiveness
Availability	Mastery	Devoutness	Shrewdness	Gentility	Efficiency
Awareness	Maturity	Dexterity	Significance	Giving	Elegance
Balance	Meekness	Dignity	Silence	Grace	Empathy
Beauty	Mellowness	Diligence	Silliness	Gratitude	Encouragement
Being the best	Meticulousness	Direction	Simplicity	Gregarious	Endurance

www.consciousfamilydynamics.com

Guidance	Mindfulness	Family	Sincerity	Growth	Energy
Happiness	Mysteriousness	Playfulness	Skilfulness	Joy	Enjoyment
Harmony	Peace	Pleasantness	Solidarity	Persuasiveness	Entertainment
Health	Perceptiveness	Pleasure	Solitude	Philanthropy	Enthusiasm
Heart	Perfection	Poise	Soundness	Success	Excellence
Helpfulness	Perkiness	Popularity	Speed	Teamwork	Excitement
Heroism	Perseverance	Potency	Spirit	Temperance	Exhilaration
Holiness	Persistence	Power	Spirituality	Thankful	Expectancy
Honesty	Utility	Practicality	Spontaneity	Thorough	Experience
Honour	Valour	Pragmatism	Spunk	Thoughtful	Expertise
Introversion	Structure	Understanding	Synergy	Transcendence	Intuition
Intensity	Wonder	Reflection	Richness	Knowledge	Intuitiveness
Intimacy	Youthfulness	Relaxation	Rigor	Investing	Inventiveness
Hopefulness	Variety	Precision	Stability	Tidiness	Modesty
Hospitality	Victory	Preparedness	Stealth	Timeliness	Motivation
Humility	Vigour	Presence	Stillness	Traditional	Neatness
Humour	Virtue	Proactive	Strength	Tranquillity	Nerve
Hygiene	Vision	Professional	Reliability	Trust	Obedience
Imagination	Vitality	Prosperity	Religiousness	Trustworthy	Open-mindedness
Impact	Vivacity	Prudence	Resilience	Truth	Openness
Independence	Warmth	Punctuality	Resolution	Uniqueness	Order
Ingenuity	Watchfulness	Purity	Resolve	Unity	Organization
Inquisitiveness	Wealth	Realism	Resourceful	Usefulness	Originality
Insightfulness	Wilfulness	Reason	Respect	Judiciousness	Outlandishness
Inspiration	Willingness	Recognition	Rest	Justice	Outrageous
Integrity	Winning	Recreation	Restraint	Keenness	Passion
Intelligence	Wisdom	Refinement	Reverence	Kindness	Supremacy

➙ *Look at all the words that you came up with above and write down the 18-24 most important words in the space below.*

Top 6 Values

→ *Now, narrow the list down again to your top 6 values. You can do this by:*

-Grouping common values into one value
-Taking out the values that are already a part of you.
-Trusting your gut instinct

1
2.
3.
4.
5.
6.

→ Get clear on what your values mean.
→ Do a video explaining what your values mean to you.
→ Video how you are going to implement it in your daily life.
→ Start telling other people what your values are and asking them what theirs are.

Blow Your Trumpet

With all the inner work we can feel that we aren't succeeding, focusing on what we are good at already is a great confidence boost. For each of the below, write the one thing you already are. E.g.: I am good at feeding my soul healthy foods. I am good at keeping my skin healthy. Ps, next time you try to say you suck at everything, pull this list out. These things will be something someone down the road completely sucks at!

For *my mind I AM*:

For *my emotions I AM*:

For *my body I AM*:

For *my soul I AM*:

Set The Bullseye

"Eye On The Prize, And You Are The Prize"

We are going to set your vision up front. What this does is it gives your brain some yummy things to focus on.

On the tough days, it may serve as a reminder that you have greater work to do, and a better life to live.

On the up days let it pull you into the vibration of your best life. I am telling you that YES, it is possible. I used to read these things; wish I had this story to tell. The story of the broken girl who grew her wings and flew.

Please don't feel far away and cut me off like I'm just some random who wrote this. I am not random. There is a reason you are reading these words. They are not mine; I am just the vessel that placed them before you. Stop doubting yourself before you pick up the ball. That's a little unfair on you and not to mention the team. We need you too. You weren't born for nothing.

On the next few pages I would like you to go into your best life. These will be your shitty first drafts. They will get clearer, better and more aligned as time goes on. Try not to decide you know your limits.

This girl, the girl who is writing this vision, it is your inner child, the girl in the mirror. Let her have a say, let it be loud.

"To Awaken We Must Believe That Something Bigger Than Us Had A Reason To Place Us On This Earth, At This Time, With This Body And These Lessons"

See Beneath Your Beautiful

What part of you do you hide, pretend not to know about, deny and push down? The part of you that has no limits and thinks you can be anything?

→*Show me, who do you dream of being. What would you be doing with your days if I had that magic wand, and time, money and judgements were of no objection? Draw a map below of you ideal day.*

This Ideal Mum

This good mum that you wish you were, I want you to imagine her in real life and tell me, how does she show up?

Describe every detail about her as a parenting when times are hard here:

Describe what she does with her children week to week:

What do her children say about her?

Now set your intention below, of who you will be as a mum.

Now list the actions steps you must take to become this woman.

What is the one thing you can do right now, this second, this instant, that can assist you in feeling a bit like this mum you just described to me? Don't write it, get up and do it.

Co-Parenting Dream

Tell me, what is your co-parenting situation like right now, and where do you want it to be? The gap, what is in there and what needs to be resolved to allow the energy to shift? There is always a way.

↦ *What is the ideal outcome, if you believed it was possible?*

↦ *What needs to be done to achieve this?*

You may need to jump over to another sheet to assist with this process, but for now, list the top 3 things that you can do to change your energy. Do you need support from a lawyer? Do you need to have that conversation with your ex? Do you need to journal a forgiveness letter in the moonlight? Do you need to do a naked cacao ceremony? You know. What is it?

↦ *What is your intention:*

Show Me The Money

I want you to go off and write a letter to money. Dear money… All the wonderful and horrible things you have ever felt about money. It's almost like a toxic boyfriend, right? Dear Money, where are you, I do everything for you and you never show up! Thank you so much I love my new shoes and lashes you are the best money ever. I hate you; you make me feel sick what happened to you the other day when I needed you? Okay, there's a clue to the relationship with money. Find a piece of paper, write the letter and then burn it. When you have finished write your new money intention here please. When you come back, fill in this page.

It is not the love of money that is evil, it is only evil that is evil. Money is as necessary as water and a good boo. Simple. Now, believing you are capable and knowing you have a wonderful relationship with money, describe to me your financial status in 5 years' time. Go as deep as you can without dictating exactly how that money comes in

Leaving On A Jetplane

Jump ahead 5 years and take a look at your life, tell me about the holidays you have had. When you went, who went with you, the weather and the adventures.

Home Dynamics Vision

School mornings for so many mums is a challenge, night times are not much better, the clothes on the bathroom floor, bedtime struggles, the breakfast dishes…the lot. It can be super stressful at home. Let us talk about the vision of what you would like your home life to look like. Describe the mornings, the evenings, the weekends. Describe the interactions. Allow yourself to believe for a moment it is achievable, because, it is.

Tane Of Your Best Life

Your lover. Your Beau. Your man. What is he like? What is the sex like, I mean does he blow your mind, or just his load? How does he greet you; does he make eye contact and smile, or come to bring the groceries in? What is he like on his phone and email? When you are upset how does he respond? What are his top 6 values in life? Where does he hang out? Tell me this man you dream of, what does he dream of? (Become what he dreams of)

Now a note. If you go off and get into a relationship before you have learnt how to be assertive, communicate, understand yourself and heal your traumas, your dream man will not manifest. The dream man belongs in your future where you have done the work. If I had the man, I wanted 12 months ago, I'd be over him by now. My growth game is too strong and fast during this stage of my life, and so too shall yours be. Do the work, become the girl that that dream man would want to be with, and he is yours.

Breast or Legs?

No health, no life. Simple. Tell me what your body and health is like in your future, 5 years' time. What do you do for exercise? What do you eat and drink? What do you wear?

Just a note on your body. During this process I would like you to make sure no matter what you are doing that your bare minimum is 2 liters of water a day, shifting energy requires water. Research into your gut health also, releasing stored energy in the body does get a reaction from the body. Set up better sleeping patters because this work changes energy, which requires energy.

White Picket Fence

It has been proven that the environment around us, our home set up, cars, work office etc., influences us. Describe to me your environment inside your 5-year vision:

\

There are things you can do right now to make that vision start to become a reality. Make it happen. Make a move.

Who Are Your Fellow Avengers?

We need social interaction, it supports us in learning, allows for the physical touch and can be pleasing on the eyes. If you could invent a new social life what would it consist of? What sort of mates do you have? Do you have parties and meetings all the time, do you have small intimate home gatherings? Do you go places, or do places come to you? What do you guys talk about? Are you comfortable naked in front of them, do you share your rejections and concerns with them? This is your dream life, don't hold back. (Ps: I would marry Tony Stark, have Thor as a client, spend wild nights in bed with Captain America and have The Hulk as my best mate.)

heartsong

BEING ME
"No Caterpillar, No Butterfly"

"As You Change

so too will the world
around you. It is law

All Of You

"The Thigh Bones Connected To The"

When we focus only on one of our parts, we neglect other parts of ourselves. Vice versa, when we neglect a part of us, other parts have to work harder to compensate and therefore we end up with aches and pains. Ever heard that saying, everything is touching everything? It is true.

Our **emotions** are our guidance system that responds to the information it perceives.

We need our **body** to move us around the earth and experience the joy of physical touch. Hugs, hair stroking, making love, pashing, holding hands.

Our **soul** is what holds the knowledge of all our times on other dimensions and is the keeper of our life's mission.

Our **minds** allow us to make sense and order of the information we receive so we can act with intelligence based on our head and our hearts. It also works to make sure we survive so the species can evolve.

We need all parts of us whilst we experience what it's like as a soul inside a body having a human experience.

Spiritual tools like crystals, oracle cards and the likes, assist us whilst we build our connection to ourselves. They smile enhance our natural abilities and serve to remind us of the power of being natural.

To ground ourselves onto this earth pane we must learn to communicate with the unseen. Life is learning experience. Regardless of what stage you are at in your awakening, be proud. Some people never wake up.

I ask you one thing, let people be who they be. While you wake up it may be so exciting to share what you now know, but nobody wants to be woken up from a slumber until they choose to. You are only their alarm clock if they ask you to be. Just be you, do you. That is enough.

Surrender To Your Soul

"You Are Not Privy To Blueprint Of The Universe"

When we get to the point where we feel like we have lost ourselves, what we have really misplaced, is the ability to trust in ourselves.

When this is happening, we stop hearing our intuition, which in turn makes us decide we don't know what to do, we become stuck, and all the while we keep trying to control everything.

Learning to surrender is not something you can be taught to do with words. It is something you must experience. It is a letting go of needing to know exactly how things are going to play out, exactly what someone else is thinking and exactly why things are the way they are.

To the universe, we are but children. We all know that children do not have clearance to know all the 'grown up' things. We allow them to know what is necessary and they surrender to trusting in our guidance. Look to the universe as your parents, guiding you. If only you would stop trying to steer the mothership, maybe you would stop crashing!

Although surrender is very much an autumn feeling, we won't make it to autumn without learning it now.

→*Think about a time in your life that you were able to let go and allow things to naturally unfold. How did you do it? What was your process:*

....
....
....
....
....
....

Holistic Wheel For Balance

"It's Just An Inch To The Left, & A Jump To The Right"

The eight sections in the wheel of life represent different aspects of life. If you are single, rate the romance section with how you feel about a relationship. In the personal growth area take into consideration your emotional wellbeing. Career can be life purpose and money is the ability to support yourself in the materialistic world.

Seeing the center of the wheel as a 1, and the outer edges as a 10, rate your level of satisfaction in each area of life by drawing a straight or curved line to create a new outer edge. The new perimeter represents your wheel of life.

Have you ever had a tyre full of bumps and uneven wear? I have and let me tell you that when my ex went to inflate it with air…it exploded. BANG. No more driving. You get the picture?

The areas that are the lowest, focus on the 1 thing you can do to lift the rating because the lowest rating is the capacity that you are currently running at. For example, if your money is at a 9/10 but your health is at a 3/10 you will only be able to average a 3/10 capacity.

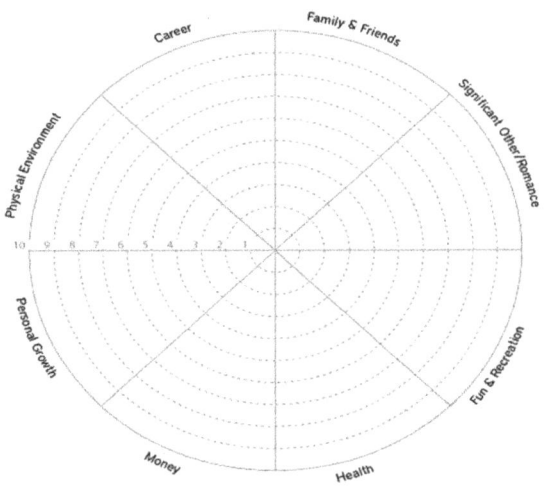

Forgiveness Wheel

"Forgiveness Is Power"

Psychologists would say forgiveness is a conscious, intentional decision to let go of the feelings that weigh a person down. Feelings of revenge, resentment, hate and/or fear towards things that have happened in the past.

When life rains problems on you, it's time to do a forgiveness wheel. The solution for most of your issues, will come down to forgiveness.

Somedays it may feel like the inner work is not practical and you should take 'real' action and get something done. That my dears is what's known as pushing and forcing. It is not the time to push when you feel impatient. Energy controls everything. Change the energy, change the outcome.

"Forgiveness Is Not Lowering Boundaries"

This exercise is a powerful exercise to shift energy. In fact, don't be surprised if you drop into your feels and feel major resistance. Just notice it and do it anyway. Lets bring forth change.

So what you will be **doing**, is writing forgiveness letters based around the areas of the balance wheel. Start with the lowest rated area and journal any resentments, regrets or blame around.

Okay here are some prompts for you to get your forgiveness wheel going. Use a fresh piece of paper and let the words just flow, then burn it.

→ *Personal Growth/Development*
Do you hold judgement against yourself for not being further ahead? For making decisions you deem stupid. Do you think you should know better already? Do you judge yourself as slow?

→ **Career & Purpose**

What do you wish you had done or had the courage to do now? What are you holding resentment toward? Have you had any bosses or colleagues treat you disrespectfully? Were you fired or have you quit from any jobs?

→ **Finances & Worth**

When have you been made to feel small and worthless? How do you feel about the color of your skin? Do you judge yourself for how you have used money in the past and present?

→ **Health & Body**

Have you been overpowered and abused? Do you have anger towards your body for failing you in any way, e.g.: Infertility, miscarriage, shape, size? Do you feel your body has rejected you in any way?

→ **Romance & Love**

Have you allowed yourself to be abused or misused in the name of love? Have you entered in as a third party to another person's relationship? Do you wish you had noticed the red flags? Do you call yourself stupid for being betrayed? Have you been betrayed? Did someone reject you?

→ **Social & Friendships**

Have you harbored resentment towards friends? Do you judge yourself for the way you have treated other friends? Have you had friends betray you?

→ **Attitude & Spirituality**

Are you mad at your god or the universe? Was there a time you believed and were let down? Do you think you missed opportunities and blame yourself for not seeing them?

→ **Family**

Do you have anger or sadness towards family members? Parents or children? What do you blame your parents for? Do you have unresolved resentments with your siblings, cousins or other family?

"Dolce Far Niente"

Vibrational Chart

No Time For Life

"The Issue Isn't The Emotion, It's Not Dealing With The Emotion"

Anxiety is when you feel a physiological and emotional reaction towards worries & fears in the future. It becomes an issue when it stops you from living your life with ease.

Thoughts come up inside our heads about things that haven't happened yet. This triggers a wave of physiological responses usually presenting inside our chests and across our hearts. Its fear. Fear that we won't have the time, energy or the capacity. Fear that we will look stupid or unprepared. Anxiety is when we go ahead to the future and conclude that we cannot do it

Can I tell you that I used to be riddled with anxiety, I used to hide in my room and not be able to breathe. I felt like a fraud, a failure and ashamed.

I couldn't even breath, which by the way is called a panic attack.

"From The Outside Looking In, My Life Was Perfect"

On the inside, I was dying of anxiety, drowning in fear. Exhausted. Paralyzed by 4 walls.

Anxiety was costing me connection, confidence, courage, clarity, money, organisation.

The payoff I was getting from anxiety was an excuse to not do the work, which by the way was overhauling my ENTIRE life. Shit it was terrifying.

The secret lies in the action you take. What you believe to be possible. How you rise after you fall. The way you think of yourself and your ability to stay in the present or return quickly when you leave.

"The Secret Is Really In Awareness And Acceptance"

The antidote to anxiety is being in the present.

When our thoughts spiral and make-up conclusions, triggers go off and emotions arise.

Here is are 2 examples of what can happen inside our minds.

Mmm that looks like a nice baby shower, my baby shower was nowhere near as good, I'm terrible at cooking, I'm hungry, we don't have any food in the fridge, oh my god just take the bottle and get off my boob I HATE breastfeeding, oh god I'm a terrible mum, shit I don't want to do this party anymore, I have so many people coming and I haven't put the rubbish out, the rooms are a mess and I need to change the sheets, man why doesn't my husband help with the fucking rubbish, I can't be bothered with soccer this weekend but I told Betty I'd take her kids too, man why do I do that I don't even like Betty and her son is so rude, oh man mums waiting for me to ring her and I can't be bothered listening to her go on about grandma today, what the fuck is the cat doing, I need to go to the supermarket, oh my goodness did I leave the hair straightener on, my hair is so ugly, omg is my husband fucking that whore-bag, that crack smoking skank, I think he is, he must think I'm so ugly now and hate how I won't party, he's going to leave me, stop this thinking it's not helping you, OMG I can't live by myself what will people say, they will laugh, God what's her face is such a bitch, what did I ever do to her, nobody likes me, ...AHHH TRIGGERED ANXIETY and FEAR!

Example 2:

Mmm that looks like a nice baby shower, my baby shower was nowhere near as good, man my sister is so mean to me she was horrible that day I can't believe she refused to move her car for me, why do my parents always take her side, am I really a bad mum, maybe it's me that's the problem I never have the house clean and dinners always late and I still need to ring the plumber......AHHH TRIGGERED HELLO ANXIETY goodbye productivity.

Just to further clarity, here is what anxiety is not.

> Anxiety is not fear
> Anxiety is not intuition
> Anxiety is not instinct
> Anxiety is not other people's energy

A lot of empaths will confuse anxiety with other people's energy or an insight they have picked up intuitively. Your intuition is about keeping you safe and is not anxiety. Learn to feel the difference between your emotions and other peoples so you can keep safe.

"I Don't Have Time For The Future"

We must get into the habit of asking ourselves what **triggered** the emotion. We can learn this by noticing our thoughts and the next section is going to cover a lot of this.

To get this in order, we must first come to know what we are dealing with. If you wrote down everything you thought and spoke to a friend the way you speak to yourself, would they still want to be friends with you afterwards.

I've just told you it's an emotion and its stemmed from our thoughts. Which means, really its under our control.

So why is it that it feels so fucking bad and leads to so much overwhelm. Why do we hide in our rooms feeling like shit and then yelling at the children because we don't have the capacity for a little question or a spilt water?

Our emotions are our guidance system and are here to support us in life. When they feel like they are ruining our life, that is when you need further support.

Social anxiety undealt with can lead us to isolating ourselves which then takes us into depression. We overwhelm ourselves with even more scenarios and suddenly we think we are now in danger of being isolated, rejected or ridiculed.

It triggers us feeling alone and not good enough. It triggers us feeling unsupported which then chucks in some good old depression, sadness and even more FEAR and BAM, there you go having a panic attack again.

"Every Emotion Serves A Purpose, Even Anxiety"

Anxiety shows up to combat procrastination. The emotion is showing you that there are things that need to be done.

What you will notice is that anxiety and overwhelm go hand in hand. This is no surprise. Inside our minds we suddenly feel that we don't have time or capacity to get things done on time, so we attach to the emotion of anxiety.

In a healthy dose, this allows us to FOCUS and get in a frenzied like state to get something done quickly and really, at the expense of all else.

So now that you realise anxiety is simply trying to help you to get things done. Ask yourself these questions: What triggered this feeling? What really needs to get done?

The question has the word "really" in it for a reason. If you don't ask the question specifically your brain will list a whole list of nonsense and loop you back around to anxiety.

"The Payoff From Anxiety Is The Adrenaline It Gives The Body"

Constantly having high adrenaline weakens your body.

Make Friends With Anxiety

- Give your anxiety visitor a name
- Put them down in a chair opposite you and imagine what they are wearing, including the color of their underwear.
- Ask them what they are here for.
- Put an age on them
- Assign them a greeting song, something funny works best

Disclaimer: I'm not a therapist, doctor or a psychologist and nothing I say should replace medical attention

Ground into the earth by visualizing roots coming from the souls of your feet. Imagine that a few feet into the earth there is a beautiful colorful crystal, which is your earth star crystal. Attach to this, feel your legs, feel the muscles of your thighs. What color are your roots? Are the deep enough and strong enough If not, visualise them going deeper and becoming stronger.

Connect to the endless wisdom of the sky. It sees everything from a higher perspective. With your eyes closed imagine from the middle of your head there is a light and it goes all the way up and connects with the infinite. What color is it? Is the connection strong enough and wide enough? How many crystals did you pass on the way up and can you send that light all the way down over the outsides of your body? Healing any sore spots along the way?

Grounding allows us to feel stable and strong.

Connection allows us to bring fun into our everyday mundane lives.

Fun allows us to listen and be present. We can listen and hear our children without the desire to hurry them up.

Being patient allows us to get into flow.

Flow heightens our intuition.

Intuition is the key to effective parenting; we can trust ourselves which means we know our families are safe.

Remember that anxiety derives from fear.

"A Mothers Intuition Is Her Most Valuable Tool, Anxiety Silences Our Intuition"

Befriending Anxiety

Anxiety is living in the future and is closely related to time and overwhelm. Notice what is happening to your breath. Close your eyes and breath. Long and deep. Walk outside and touch a tree, touch the earth, smell the air, ground.

Describe what you are feeling:

Where are you feeling it, in your body?

What has triggered it?

What are you afraid to admit?

What would happen if you admitted it?

Do you know this to be a fact or is it an assumption?

What do you need to do to move towards a happier life?

Befriending Anxiety

All we truly have is here and now and the stories in our heads. Even those stories are happening in the now. Breath is life. When we do not breathe, we tell our body to activate its stress system. Breathing can be done anywhere anytime, and no one ever got in trouble for breathing.

The box breathing technique is used by the military before battle. It keeps you focused yet grounded. I use it most days. Please practice it now.

Breath into the count of 4, hold 4, breath out for 4, hold 4. (Repeat) In for 4, hold 4, out 4, hold 4. In for 4, hold 4, out 4, hold 4. In for 4, hold 4, out 4, hold 4. Repeat.

Note: If you are wanting to go to sleep make your out breath is longer than your in breath.

Describe what you are feeling:

Where are you feeling it, in your body?

What has triggered it?

What are your concerns & fears?

What are the facts?

STOP: Touch something, smell something, notice what you can see, notice what you can hear. Come back to the present moment.
What can you do right now to make the situation better?

What is the priority?

What actually needs doing?

Befriending Anxiety

Anxiety is created first in your mind. Catch the trigger, notice the thoughts, breathe through them. It gets easier.

What emotion is the strongest?

What color is the emotion?

What body part can I use to let it out?

What did it want to tell me?

What story did I make up to get triggered?

What can I do to connect to my breath and nature right now?

What is the priority?

What can I commit to?

Befriending Anxiety

A lot of what we think we must get done is only so that we look like we have our shit together to the judgmental world. Here's an idea, keep the judgmental people out of your world. It is after all, your world.

I am feeling:

I can feel it in the body around my:

I was triggered by:

What am I doing just to 'look' good to other people?

Is it working for me?

What can I let go of to allow myself more time?

What is stopping me from letting go?

Write below your action plan to work through this trigger. Be realistic.

Befriending Anxiety

The awareness of what is happening inside is the best place to start when our thoughts are out of control and we feel like life is hard, horrible and that we aren't good enough. We must get into the habit of asking ourselves what triggered the emotion. We can learn this by noticing our thoughts.

Describe what you are feeling:

Where is the emotion stored in your body?

What was happening in the moment you were triggered?

Do you feel capable, supported and secure?

STOP: Touch something, smell something, notice what you can see, notice what you can hear. Come back to the present moment.

What can you do to feel capable? List the steps here.

Befriending Anxiety

The awareness of what is happening inside is the best place to start when our thoughts are out of control and we feel like life is hard, horrible and that we aren't good enough. We must get into the habit of asking ourselves what triggered the emotion. We can learn this by noticing our thoughts.

Describe what you are feeling:

Where are you feeling it, in your body?

What has triggered it?

What are your concerns & fears?

What are the facts?

STOP: Touch something, smell something, notice what you can see, notice what you can hear. Come back to the present moment.
What have you done in the past that worked?

What is the priority?

Emotion V's Feeling

"We Are Not All Cut From The Same Cloth"

An emotion is the response to the perceived information around us.

Feeling is the conscious awareness of the emotion.

Everybody has emotions, not everybody feels. These people may be labeled as 'heartless' 'cruel' or described as 'lacks empathy." They simply are uneducated in recognizing the emotion and being able to name it, let alone describe it.

"I Didn't Know That I Felt Like That Until It Was Too Late"

There is a book called 'The Art Of Empathy", written by Karla McLaren. It is the most fantastic book and has been a huge framework for my understanding how to act on what emotion.

Emotions are not something we can escape or control. We can only change the way we perceive the world around us. This is what our emotions process.

For me, being an empath and an intuitive means that I have always had a strong ability to understand how another is feeling to the point that I could feel the feeling. I can jump into another person's emotions far easier than they can, even when they are miles apart from me. This is deeper spiritual work and not something I cover much in this book.

For example, if I have a client who has not cried and is in a situation where they need to let go and are constantly being hurt, I will feel that sadness. I will cry if they don't. I used to despise this and consider it a weakness. Shit, sometimes I couldn't go anywhere because I could feel everyone's feels

The game changer for me was saying "I am aware of other people's energy"

"When I Was Pregnant, I Could Feel My Unborn Babies Dislike Of Crowds"

I have dreams about other people, I lucrative dream and I feel when other people throw their energy on me. I bring this up because maybe you do too. Everyone receives their messages differently and I would get a lot of dreams because I didn't hear the message during the waking hours. Well, to be honest I did hear them, I ignored them.

You will receive yours in the way you are most receptive. I had a friend that I would dream about, I knew he could do with someone to listen to him, but it was awkward for me to say, hey, I dream about you and I know things.

I learnt how to manage this by learning how to manage myself, relationships, communication and becoming a coach.

Now I get beautiful dreams with very clear messages. I don't often dream of others now because I receive and hear my guidance during the waking moments and act on it straight away and ask them what it means to them.

As I have been writing this book, I have had many messages for woman and reached out to them. It doesn't surprise me how many say to me that my timing and message is impeccable. It is not my message or timing, (although my ego loves it), it's me communicating on behalf of the guidance they have asked for.

"Learn To Recognize When You Have An April In Your Life. Learn To Recognize, When You Are The April In Someone's Life"

I know that being in my empath energy is powerful. My visions are clearer, my lessons are gentle. I believe this is something we all have access to and once we learn empathy with boundaries, we learn how to not let it drain us.

> *"It Is True Feminine Power To Be Intuitively Awake"*

To manage life as an empath and thrive in it, you must learn to understand your own intuitive gifts.

Lets cover some basic perceptions on emotions now.

Anger - Respect My Authoritah

"Something Has Crossed My Boundary"

Angers Message: Assert yourself. There is a boundary that has been crossed and I am finding it unacceptable. I will continue to show up if you do not implement a healthy boundary and learn to communicate assertively. I may show up when you watch events that have nothing to do with me because I feel that it is not ok for that person to get away with it. I will need you to learn to stay in your own energy and not focus on the news and other people's problems.

Ask Yourself: What behavior have I allowed that I need to take responsibility for? What am I protecting?

"I Am Practising Being Assertive"

Guilt – I Am Wrong

"I've Decided I Am A Bad Human"

Guilts Message: I feel like a bad person because this goes against my values and morals. I feel that what I have done is ill behavior and I know better. I feel horrible.

Ask Yourself: What values have I stepped on? How can I amend the situation and restore the balance? How can I know that I am not my behavior, I am not a bad person I simply behaved poorly? What can I do to strengthen my values?

"I Am Implementing My Values"

Shame – I Don't Accept It

"I've Done Something Against My Values"

Shames Message: My behavior was not something I am proud of. I care what those people or person thinks about it. It is not who I am.

Ask Yourself: Who have I hurt and how can I amend the situation? What led me to the behavior and how can I prevent it? How can I let go of the shame?

"I Am Learning, Its Ok To Learn"

Sadness – I Am Hurting

"So Long, Farewell, It's Time To Say Goodbye"

Sadness's Message: I've come because you and I both know it is time to let go and move on. If you don't let go now, I will elevate into grief. I am ready to let go. This isn't right for me anymore.

Ask Yourself: What or who do I need to let go of? Do I need to cry? How can I let go?

"I Am Learning How To Trust My Autumn Process"

Envy – I Deserve It More

"It's Not Fair, Why Do They Have It And I Don't"

Envy's Message: I show up when I feel that materialistic things or recognition type things cannot be mine. It's not about the other person, it's because you don't feel capable. Sometimes someone has what you worked for and I feel mad about it because I still want it. I just need you to get to work on getting us what we really desire.

Ask Yourself: How can I feel capable? Does something need to be made right? "Trust That No Matter What Happens, You Will Be Ok"

"I Am Capable, Look At How Far I Have Come"

Apathy – I Don't Want To Feel

"I Don't Want To Feel A Damn Thing"

Apathy's Message: There is too much that just happened. I need time out or you are going to lose the plot and act terribly. Stop. If we do not stop, I will go to anger.

Ask Yourself: What am I hiding? What is the truth of my upset? How do I separate myself and put in boundaries?

"I Am In A Safe Place To Feel"

Grief – Death Is Essential

"Something Has Died, Is This Real"

Griefs Message: Life includes death. It is a natural process. Allow yourself to feel the full spectrum of emotions, move through them. Do not stay here with me, I will make life horrible. Just go through all the feelings and I am gone. This is not something that can be rectified.

Ask Yourself: How can I accept the ending?

"I Am Greatful For The Memories"

Hatred – Shadow Work

"I Hate In Others, What I Refuse To See In Me"

Hatreds Message: Undealt with envy and anger can turn into hatred, but we cannot hate in others that which we like in ourselves. Meaning, we hate in others the reflection of what we hate in ourselves, (side note: I found hatred the most challenging emotion to understand. Deeper work in hatred is required. Perceptions and reflections of others)

Ask Yourself: What do I hate about myself? What is the link?

"Love Hate Relationships Are Based On Unresolved Pain"

Situational Depression – It's Dark

"I Can't Do This Anymore"

The Message: I'm a messenger from your soul. Please stop. For the love of God, fucking stop. Let go. Move on. Grieve. Just stop trying to fix this situation. It's done.

Ask Yourself: What am I wasting my energy on? How can I return to the girl in the mirror? What am I on this earth for?

"I Am Alive To Fufil A Puropose"

Jealousy – Back Off Its Mine

"Don't Steal My Sausage, It's The Only One Left"

The Message: I show up when I am worried that something that I think keeps me safe is about to be taken or could be taken. I have a bad rep, yet all I want it to keep my home a home. Usually I show up without warrant if you don't feel worthy or stable in your relationships. I just need you to feel stable and secure in your relationships.

Ask Yourself: How can I feel stable? How can I grow my self-worth? What betrayal needs healing?

"I Am Capable Of Supporting Myself"

Fear – Staying Alive

"I Do Not Want To Die"

Fears Message: I am fear and I am real. I can take over your entire body depending on how I assess the situation. You programmed me to keep you safe. Back in the day I would show up when things like tigers or snakes were present. Id show up when our villages were ransacked and attacked. Now I show up when someone doesn't like your shoes, or your eyebrows. I show up when a man stares at your breasts or speaks in a deep voice. It feels the same to me. I must keep you alive and being accepted keeps you part of the tribe. Without the tribe we will die alone in the cold of the paddocks. What I need is for you to change direction or behavior and remove yourself from danger. Oh, and if your shoes aren't really danger, I would need you to reprogram me. I am your friend; I keep you alive. Stop hating on me and just tell me how you want me to operate. PS: If you don't address me, I will turn into panic.

Ask Yourself: What do I need to do? What do I need to change?

"Being Comfortable Being Unhappy, Is A Sign Of Self Hate"

Fuck You To The Man

"Goodbye My Lover, Goodbye My Friend"

Can I just say I miss anger! I know that sounds tragedy, but it was my best friends for years and it really made me feel powerful at times. What a trip.

I gave up anger because it had moved to hatred, and anger asked me to let it go. I had spent the night off chops being white girl wasted and oh the shame I felt. Apparently, I had told people I hated my ex-husband but the sex was amazing and I miss it. Not my finest moment.

So, what about when we are done with the anger? When we realise its barricaded us from speaking through love. That we cannot be love whilst we are being with anger. Anger is devoid of love. Hatred is devoid of love.

Saying goodbye to anger if it has been your default go to emotion is seriously courageous! Underneath it you will meet sadness. She's a soft feminine emotion and my goodness the things I must report about sadness.

Ok so, write a letter telling that person or thing all the ways in which they have angered you, and well, fuck you! Fuck you to hell and back.

Let me clarify a couple of things first.

1- You may not get to release it all in one go. Sorry. Each time gets easier and quicker.
2- It won't look the way you think it should look. It's not pink guys and there are no unicorns.
3- No one will praise you for it.
4- It most likely will hurt. How much, and how long is up to how much you surrender.
5- You will try to distract, run and hide from the feminine sadness when she shows up. Just be with here. She's actually nice.

Express what you like how you like, as gangster or pussy as you like. All your feels. Express them. No one else should bear witness to this. For a few reasons. Energy released is for the universe to transmute it into love. It is not to be weighed on another empath's shoulders. It is not to be spoken of over and over and swam in. It is to be taken from your mind, through your hands and out of your body. Poof.

Please do not use sex, alcohol, food or anything else after this to make yourself feel better. If you are sharing your energy with anyone else directly after this notice if you are being avoidant and hindering your growth.

Your letter can be to one person or to multiple people. This is not a letter where you write the things they did well or justify the things they did.

This is to pour out the feelings and thoughts you have that align with anger and hate. This is not the time to pretend you don't have these thoughts.

"Vomit It Onto That Paper"

The guidance:

> There are no rules, the universe is in charge here
>
> Do not control anything. It is about surrender and release
>
> For your eyes only
>
> You may like to pray or set an intention. "God, please allow me full expression and to guide me to the way that best serves me to release anything that is holding me in a low vibration. Please take the negativity and transmute it into love"
>
> Be alone for at least 2 hours, ideally the night.
>
> Put your phone away

Do not fuse with the story. If you get mad, shake it off, step back, drink some water and go again

Start how you like, but ideally use the most common fuck you phrase in your head. e.g.: I hate you. I despise you. You make my skin crawl.
Keep it moving, we are expressing thoughts and emotions not the story.

Keep going until you break down in a soft cry that is coming from the softness of your heart. Hello sadness.

Allow all the feels to come up to the surface in your body, and then allow them to come out through your hands, your eyes, your breath.

Whilst in the soft feminine sadness, acknowledge her. Notice that it's been some time since you felt her and know that she is a step higher in the vibration ladder to fulfillment. She is your nurture. She came to emotionally hug you and tell you that she will never leave you.

LET HER IN. Sit with her. Let the hot tears come out of your heart.

Once you have allowed the feelings to come up you can then proceed in the way you usually would. Be it journaling, meditation, swimming, a shower, exercise. Burning sage and Palo Santo. Dancing or simply sleeping.

Be prepared to feel a little more vulnerable, stay in your heart. May love lead the way.

"Listen To Your Soul, She Will Protect You,

If You Only Listen"

Energy In Motion

All our emotions are here for a reason. Think about it. Do you think we were given the ability to feel this range of emotions by accident? The issue is that no one really knew how to work with them before. Everyone chases this happiness feeling, yet its set us up to fail.

Feelings are super intelligent. Start to first notice what you are feeling and to put a name against it. From there you can start to notice which ones you avoid and why, how to learn to accept them and not get stuck in them, and to then use them to your advantage.

What is the emotion I am experiencing?

Name it:

Where in my body can I feel it?

What triggered it?

What is it trying to teach me?

What else is it trying to teach me?

What value of mine is upset and needs restoring?

How can I allow it to process and be released?

What is the lesson I am learning?

Never underestimate the power of nature to heal, especially water.

Energy In Motion

Name it to tame it is a way to bring awareness into what we are experiencing. When we name an emotion, it allows the emotion to simmer down and for us to work with it, rather than against it. Please do some work around learning what emotions are about. All our emotions, even the ones we don't want, are valuable.

Name the emotion that keeps you awake at night:

Where in the body do you feel it?

What is the story you have made up?

And the conclusion?

What is it you must get done to let the emotion know you have understood its message?

Energy In Motion

As your emotions arise, it is your job to allow them to be released. Do not stuff them down into your body. That is how you get aches and pains. Emotions are energy in motion. All energy needs to move. If you do not allow your emotion its movement it will sit inside your body and cause dis-ease.

This is a process. It is different for everyone. Emotions play out the same for us all, our process is always different. Use the elements, the sea, the moon, the bush, the fire to guide you. And of course, your emotions.

How do I react to sadness?

Do I cry?

When was the last time I allowed myself to cry?

What was the reason I allowed it?

How do I feel about crying?

How do I react to anger and hatred?

What is my pattern?

What do I think about people who display rage and anger?

Research anger and sadness and record here 3 things you learnt about each emotion.

1.
2
3.
4.
5.
6.

What lessons am I learning about myself?

Now would be a great time to look for a spiritual healer. One who empowers you rather than enables you. Someone to clear the energy from your etheric body.

Energy In Motion - Children

Our children want to feel a connection with us more than anything. We are their stability in life. What we need you to do is to forgive every time you yell, every time you weren't present or fed them noodles for dinner. It is not helpful for you or the children to hold this emotion. Write a forgiveness letter to yourself, check my blog for guidance. Colin Tipping writes a book called Radical Forgiveness; it is life changing.

Again, use your intuition, your guides, the earths elements and the moons energy to boost the forgiveness ceremony.

What does connection mean to you?

How connected do you feel to yourself?

How connected to each one of your children do you feel?

What can you do to connect with your child, 5 minutes a day per child?

What does the perfect mother look like, sound like, act like, smell like and dress like?

How can you become her?

How else?

Please make sure you are getting yourself to workshops, retreats, healers, coaches and the likes. Human connection is important.

Energy In Motion - Mumlife

Conscious parenting requires us to be conscious first. We must fill our own cups in order to be able to fully be there with our children. As you heal, let them see the winter and autumn process only to the point that they can cope with it. If you let them see you cry, tell them it will be okay, and let them see you wipe your eyes and eventually fall in love again. Yes, you will allow love again one day my girl because, oh my goodness, feeling desired by a man from a conscious state is fucking all the goods!

Like I've said, I came back for YOU. I can feel you when you read this, weird isn't it. I want you to know, you are not alone. I am here. I may have walked before you, but right here where you stand in this energetic space, I am here with you. Keep going. You are doing better than you give yourself credit for. I know. I know more about you than you realise. I know the end goal...better...not bitter. xo

When was a time you felt connected with the kids in the past, what were you doing?

What does intimacy mean to you?

What do my children really desire from me? What do they ask for?

What is missing from my home environment and how can I balance that out?

How can I be more peaceful in my home?

How can I allow more of my feminine side to come through?

You were not born with a parenting manual. Give yourself a break. All that matters now, is that you are committed to your growth for the good of the family. Oh, and for your information, your intuition IS your parenting manual.

Energy In Motion - Mumguilt

One of the biggest challenges with parenting through separation after betrayals is the mum guilt. Most mums feel strong emotions about the any mistress, the friends who knew the secret, the father of the child etc. It is common for mums to not want this horrible woman or people around their child. Who the hell would?

The fact of the matter is, research shows that it is usually advantageous for the child to spend time with both parents. This is where your intuition must be stronger than your ego. We must address your guilt and underlying emotions so that you can tap into your intuition and do what is at the best interests for your little humans. Use this template to go deeper on how to shift the emotions.

What triggered the guilt?

When else do you feel this?

When was the first time you ever felt this feeling?

What are the thoughts you are thinking?

Who in your lifetime has told you those things about yourself?

What are your perceived weaknesses in parenting?

How can you parent from a space of love and acceptance? Faith, trust and pixie dust? What are you not seeing?

I encourage you to ask the universe to guide you towards connection with your children. Everything comes back to connection. I cannot stress this enough. Any time you have challenges in your home I would stake my life on the fact that there is a break in the connection. This is true even when external unfathomable things have happened to our children, if you connect with them, they find the strength to move through and not stay stuck in the trauma. Connect. Connect when you want to scream. Connect when you feel the love. Connect when you are stressed. There is always time for cuddles. Make this a priority in your home if you would like more peace.

Energy In Motion

What have you learnt so far?

Jealousy shows up because:

What I can do to allow jealousy to be released is:

Apathy is:

What is good about envy?

I am most jealous when:

The story I have attached to the people I am jealous about is:

I first created the story when:

The gift of jealousy is:

The gift of apathy is:

Envy shows up to tell me:

Things I now know about myself and these emotions:

winter

PART: GOING IN

"No Pain, No Gain"

"I Don't Like

the pain, she says.

Nobody does,

he says."

Winter Needs Nurture

"Come Inside; Take Shelter From The Storm"

Winter is a time to introvert.

We have been brought to the winter season to find the truth, our truth. It is a time of surrender, a time to go within, retreat from what the world expects and to strip back the masks you wear.

In the winter season what you need is hope, faith and love. To survive the cold nights, we need to know that the warmth is coming, that the sun will return.

This is the time of the feminine, the allowance, the nurture, the being, the flexing. This is not a time for the masculine, it is not the time to rip things apart and make sudden movements.

It is the time for observation. It is the time for you to stop and feel where you are and what led you to this spot.

Winter is associated with hands. A mother's hands are nurturing, supportive and healing. These are the hands that guide, hands that lead you to the clearing in the woods. Ask the universe to send you hands that lift you up in your time of need.

Learn to surrender and seek alternative perspectives. It is time for you to start to become mindful, to notice what you think and what you make everything mean.

Winter is the time to see what we expect of others, how we show up in our communication, how we benefit from shitty situations even when we say we don't.

Welcome to winter, it is time to conversate with the girl in the mirror. Please make yourself a warm cup of tea and listen to her. Hear what she has to say without interruption.

…Suivez-Moi – Follow Me.

Call In Friends & Support

"It Takes A Village To Raise Consciousness"

Start calling in your people. A coach, a bunch of books, the naughty friend, the morally sound friend, a past life worker, a healer or 4, a guy mate, a lawyer, the cheerleader friend, the been there done that friend and the friend with kids to entertain your kid.

As you know, at the start of my transformation I hired a private coach. I was ready to do the work. Don't get me wrong, I was scared shitless and still wanted to save my marriage.

"Bonds Are Created When We Go Through Something Tough Together"

If you could imagine our emotional homes had 4 pillars on which our best life was laid out on, it would be these.

Support +- Clarity +- Connection = Empowerment.

Support brings the courage you are seeking. I had a reiki healer, a shamanic healer and a consistent psychic reader. I have put all their details on the website for you. Your intuition will tell you who is right for you at each stage.

I attended workshops, retreats, breath work workshops, yoga classes, boot camps and leadership training. I completed my Usui Reiki 1, started a life coaching diploma. Attended woman's anti-violence program as the victim, attended parenting through separation, got a lawyer and read trillions of books. Hear the calling and go. Decide.

"Just As Leaders Recognise Leaders, People In Growth Recognise People In Growth"

Your Inner Be

"Who Wears The Pants, Who Really Cares?"

A lot of us are playing the role of the wonderful mum who lets her kids participate in everything. The most common response to people is "I'm so busy" followed up with all the things you "have" to do. Nothing bores me faster than someone listing all the things they "have" to do when they are running their 'busy' story. It's a pattern. Learn to recognise the payoff and find a way to simplify and be okay doing sweet fuck all.

There is a book called "Busy As Fuck" by Karen Nimmo. It's a great read for those of you who find you say "I've been so busy" often. The goal is "I've been so …productive, content, inspired, peaceful" …not busy.

Doing is a masculine trait.

> ## "Masculinity Dominates And Leaves Little Room For Femininity To Shine Through"

Femininity is the part of us that nurtures our newborns, is gentle with the children and is 'clucky' when another baby is around. This is the part of us that lets someone offload while we listen without trying to fix things. I was so far in my masculine that I absolutely could not just listen, I thought it was a waste of my time and would always try to solve the problem.

Our feminine comes through when we feel safe. We must find a way to let our brains know that we are not in danger. The fear is not valid. This alone can truly change our family dynamics.

There are a lot of ways we can do this including understanding brain science and survival mode. I encourage you to study the book "The Whole Brain Child" by Daniel J Siegel and Tina Bryson. This shows a lot about our brains and you will recognise how you also be fire off your amygdala in times that you are not truly in danger.

For now, we will focus on feminine energies and learning to go deeper with our intuition. I will show you some day to day ideas on the next page.

Getting In Touch With 'Her'

"How Do You Take Your Tea Dear"

1. Honor your sexuality as sacred, flirt don't tease.
2. Allow yourself to be chased by the masculine.
3. Move your body in a feminine way.
4. Sleep in the nude and honor your nakedness as a woman.
5. Listen to soft romantic music.
6. Breath slowly and deeply while you orgasm.
7. Allow people to give to you. Receive.
8. Intuitively create. Get the crafts out. Pull up Pinterest and do some DIY things. Let your intuition guide the way. Creation is feminine. After all, we do create babies inside our wombs.
9. Flowers. Bring nature inside.
10. Create a fluffy romantic place to relax in.
11. Decorate your bedroom with sensual art. Beautiful abstract couples making love in soft sepia. Sensual and sexy.
12. Choose kinder nicer words. Soft descriptive words with pause and a soft tone.
13. Accept compliments. This is part of receiving. And learn to flirt. To smile softly with your eyes, to gently toss your hair, to tilt your head to the side when listening to a man.
14. Learn to walk gracefully. Think of the woman with the baby in her arms. Its gentle and exudes love.
15. Nurture. Make time for hugs. Think head on the bosom of the breast. Stroke their hair. Gently touch their cheek. Kiss the forehead. Gently stroke their arms or back. Make chicken soup. Bake some cookies. Run a hot bath.

What She Looks Like

Imagine chin and eyes slightly down, hair in the sunlight with big soft curls, warm colors. Imagine plaits and flowers. Daisy chains.

Flowy materials, girly colors like pink, lavenders, plums, apricots – Imagine florals. luxurious, feminine fabrics like silk, chiffon, velvet, satin, cashmere and lace

Long skirts and dresses – imagine bohemian, flow mixed with lace.

Soft pink lipsticks – Imagine gentle flirty smiles, shiny lips and dimples.

Soft natural make-up – imagine natural and accentuated. Imagine eyelashes batting and gloss. Imagine browns and apricots.

What She Feels Like

- Sensual
- Empathetic
- Emotional
- Gentle
- Motherly
- Creative
- Present
- Warm
- Kind
- Acceptance
- Intuition
- Receptive
- Soft
- Allowing

Boundaries

"Vampires Can Only Come In, If You Invite Them Over The Threshold"

Love, which by default is unconditional, does not mean that we have to accept shitty behavior.

Just because we don't like the way someone is treating us, doesn't automatically mean we stop loving them. Just because someone puts a boundary up, doesn't mean they automatically don't love us.

Love is not relationships. Love is love. Relationships are relationships.

"A Boundary Is A Line In The Sand That States The Conditions Of Entry."

Here are a couple of examples.

1- In my home it is unacceptable to allow men that I may have a sexual relationship or anything that is not platonic into my home when Addison is in the house. Irrespective of if she is awake or asleep. **Because** her safety is my priority and I never want her to grow up and think, my mother was a hoe. (Trust me, I hear this often.) It is simple to implement. It's just not an option. For those who may now ask well what about the solo mum thing when I have no support and I have needs too? I would ask you to investigate what need it is that this sex is giving you? Especially if it is a man you do not know. Your work is in how you seek to fill the voids, not in how to get laid. I practiced chastity. The first time I failed my 12-week goal at 11 weeks and 5 days. The next time I did 5.5 months. And now I'm far more interested in my book than boys.

2- Another boundary I have is how I speak with my male friends. When I share stories with them about my sex life, I will speak only in clinic type terms. For example, I will say sex, not fuck. I will keep my tone neutral and not allow the energy of the event to transfer. I won't go into how my body felt in descriptive words. **Because**, I respect our friendship and I am very aware of how men are visual and a simple few words can turn a conversation into something sexual. I treasure my friendships and some of the men I know now were crucial to my understanding of my ex-husband. Their friendship allowed me to understand and forgive. I would never disrespect that by using the power of the pussy to manipulate the conversation just to have a quick fix. I don't need every man on the planet to find me attractive. (P.S: I learnt this by doing the opposite and then feeling ashamed that I had pushed his boundary, full well knowing what I was doing, just so I could feel a moment of satisfaction.)

3- Another boundary I have is gossip. I won't listen to people put people down. Sometimes people have things going on in their lives and want to get into the 'he's a complete idiot' sort of talk. I will allow it for a moment as they need a quick vent but that is it. I will then speak up and state, ok, let's get back on topic. It doesn't feel good to speak like this. What is it that is affecting you? Therefore, my friends know I am not the one you come to, to gossip about people.

Are you starting to see? Start to notice what you negotiate on an what you do not. This will give you a clue on whether you need to put boundaries up. Boundaries are not barricading your heart. Your values will support your implementing boundaries.

"Boundaries Do More Than Show People What You Stand For, They Keep You Standing"

They will repel people who do not wish to respect you and they will attract people who respect you.

Boundaries are an absolute if you feel like you are a doormat. In my next book I will tell you why I went deep into boundaries after being called a doormat by my ex-husband's mistress. Shit did it cut deep. I had no boundaries. I had no sign on my door at all.

A boundary is a limit, it's saying hey, here is the line you will not cross it. If you do there is an effect, the effect is I may no longer open my door for you. Even if I love you, I will love you from over here. I am worth this much. I will only be spoken to in this manner. I will be treated only in this way. I will allow only this into my life. Any mess I make in my life is because I chose to allow it over the line.

Everything is my responsibility because the boundaries I have are self-made.

You might actually be surprised by what your boundaries truly are. One of mine is promises. If you make a promise to me, you must keep it. Irrespective of what it was. I have a very strong boundary of 'make promises sparingly, keep them faithfully.' If this boundary gets crossed, I will make the time to have that conversation with the person. Even if I feel awkward.

There is a line, you crossed it. Let's make that line crystal clear so you understand that it is there, and we can move forward. Cross it again I will naturally be repelled by you.

When you start to really put a stake in the grounds your emotions will rise, and you will find yourself exerting energy. It can be exhausting. What I want you to do is really feel into your ancestors. Where do you derive your strength from? Feel that energy and allow the unseen to support you while you learn to rise. Why expect other people to keep a boundary that even you do not keep?

"Boundaries Without Action Are Actually Self Betrayal"

What Is On Your Door

Imagine you have a door to your life. On that door are the conditions of entry. Your negotiables and non-negotiables. What you will tolerate and what you will not tolerate. The sort of person you will get into bed with and the sort of person you won't engage with.

If you had to sum it up on an A4 sign, what would be on your door sign?

Conditions of entry:

Be Assertive

"Let Your Yes Be A Yes And Your No Be A No"

Being assertive means maintaining your boundaries in a respectful manner. When we are assertive, we save ourselves from getting angry.

Passive behavior means we do not stick up for ourselves. Being passive can sometimes have people feeling like they do not know where they stand with you, so they walk around feeling nervous. Is this ok, is this not ok? Your behavior is confusing for them. Passive parents may believe they are giving their children what they want, I believe the child are confused about who guides them.

Aggressive behavior means we stick up for ourselves in an overbearing way which can make people feel scared of us. People parent aggressively and then believe their children are well behaved. I believe their children are controlled by fear.

Being assertive sits in the middle of the 2 and sounds like a respectful request or directive. People quickly learn who you are and what you are about and then can choose to be around you or not. With the children, they know how you operate and can learn how to practice being assertive with you and other people. Being assertive does not mean you are stubborn. It means you are clear with your intentions and limits.

Here is 3 quick examples of a response to little 10 year old Johnny saying he does not want to go to bed even though it is 7pm, his bedtime. He says he is hungry and will refuse to sleep.

Passive – Oh, well I suppose you can have some potato chips and watch a movie. (Later, at 10pm you get mad and yell at Johnny because its so late and you didn't get down time and everything is his fault. You go to bed with Mumguilt. Johnny is learning that if someone loves you, they let you do whatever you like.)

Aggressive – Get into bed right now and do not answer me back or I will take all your new cars off you! GET! NOW! (Once you simmer down you feel mean and go in and give Johnny some food, talk to him and try to make your guilt disappear. Johnny is learning that love is aggressive and that disrespect, fear and raised voices equals love.)

Assertive – Johnny it is bedtime at 7pm. It is now 7pm. You are to go to bed and stay in bed. You may not get up. You are welcome to have a big breakfast in the morning. This is not negotiable. (Anything further Johnny says, you repeat this. You feel fine because you stated the boundary and did not negotiate on a non-negotiable. Johnny stops making these sorts of requests because he is learning that there are some things that he can not push around.)

Here is a phrase that can assist you in being assertive with your friends and other adults.

"Thank You, No Thank You"

Here's a task for the week to practice assertion.

No justifying
No blaming
No excusing

An example would be if someone invites you to a lunch and you don't want to go. Usually you would be passive and go anyway and then later be annoyed at all the things you had to do still. Or, you would be aggressive and tell them all the reasons you cannot go and be annoyed at them for even asking.

So, the idea is to be grateful for the invite and to politely say no. Thank you, no thank you.

If people respect you, they won't push at you. People will react to changes in your behavior and may at first take it personally, so allow some kindness and space.

Remember, do not justify, excuse or blame. Now we will talk about limbo relationships.

On A Train Bound For Nowhere

"You Can Get Off At Any Station"

Foreword: For the purpose of this article I will define limbo as being a period of more than 2 weeks in a relationship where you live together, 3 weeks where you do not, and 4 weeks for a long-distance relationship.

Relationship limbo is when you are waiting on the other party to decide if there is a relationship or not. You are trying to be patient during a time when you are the most impatient you have ever been. Nothing feels stable in limbo, because, nothing is.

Many mistrusts arise. You may have violence, abuse and major disrespect. Or you may simply have hot and cold emotions. Tears, desperation, promises and desire. Break downs, late night messages and the words 'we are done' said over and over.

The sex may improve, or it may die off.

"Our Bodies Are Dying To Be Savaged And Screaming To Be Held And Caressed In Love"

Every night spent together, you wonder, 'is this the last time?' One minute you are thinking you could never be with another, the next fantasising about the man who gave you a sideways glance at the supermarket.

Either way, in relationship limbo we are sitting in what feels like a prison, screaming for someone or something to let us out. Tell us what to do, where to aim and how to fix this. We make promises to do better and we take on all the blame. I love you. I can't ever love another. You just want your life back.

The rollercoaster that comes with limbo is excruciating and literally nauseating. The made-up thoughts. The derailing. The waiting in line. One minute everything seems fine, just like normal. The next, your sobbing in your bed feeling like your chest is about to explode. Your crying weak at the bottom of the shower while your eyes feel like razor blades. Your yelling at the kids. Your wide awake at 3am. Your dry retching at 6am in the morning.

It is a jail cell we put ourselves in because we don't believe that life can be better without them. We believe it is worth waiting for, fighting for. We do not have the self-worth, self-love or respect we need to pull ourselves up.

"Our Cup Is Empty"

Let's cover a few of the action steps that are needed to put ourselves first:

1. **Live Apart** - If you are not in a committed relationship, do not live together. Someone who is worth it will commit to you and have no trouble working out what he wants.

2. **No Nookie** - Ladies, keep your legs closed and men, keep it in your pants.

3. **Do You** - There is no such thing as "I need time," "I'm confused." Translate those into, 'Just do you!" A person in love does not need more than a couple of weeks to figure themselves out.

4. **Go MIA** - Cut the contact for a couple of weeks. Do not be available for someone who is not available. If you have children speak only of the necessities and be mindful of using the kids as an excuse to speak. 2 weeks is nothing compared to living in limbo for endless weeks. I wish I had had the means to do this. Space makes a difference.

5. **Custody** - Get the custody sorted from the outset and have it made legal whilst you are both still amicable. If things change, it is very difficult to know what your heart is and what is your pain.

6. **Say No** - Stop doing the people and the things you do not love so that you can make way for the things you do like and love. Remove from your life all the things you detest and do only out of obligation.

7. **Journal** - Journal your thoughts.

8. **Use Music** - Sing love songs to yourself. Dance. Sing and Dance.

"The Secret To Surviving' Is Knowing' What To Throw Away And Knowing' What To Keep"

One thing that can be challenging is stopping the sex and communication.

"Tripped, Fell, Landed On His Dick?"

There are so many excuses we hold on to this. It's familiar, no one else knows how I like it, I haven't been with anyone else for so long, I want to stick it to the bitch, it means we are still close, it means he still loves me, it makes me feel desirable…

What's your excuse? You are going to need a really big 'why', to make this a reality. We will cover more about sex on the next page.

I will stop having sex with such and such because:

"How Can I Be My Future Self Now?"

Who Will You Be?

Who will you be now? Who do you desire to be? What will you be like? How will you show up? How will you feel? For each of the below, write the one thing you will become. *E.g.: For my mind I am practicing observing my thoughts. For my emotions I am learning more about anger.*

→ *For my mind **I AM**:*

→ *For my emotions **I AM**:*

→ *For my body **I AM**:*

→ *For my soul **I AM**:*

Making Stories Up

Inside our heads we make up stories. All day long, every day.

We make up a picture of what something will look like. When that doesn't eventuate the way our heads designed we find ourselves making it mean something which triggers an emotion. If we cannot pause, we act on the emotion and thus, create mess in our lives.

Pay Offs

Every thought we have and every action we take, gives us something; a **payoff** that our brain believes is helpful.

Your job is to figure out what it is that you 'get' from the unhelpful thought and to write it down. It easy for us to know what things are costing us, the deeper work is figuring out what benefit we get from it.

"Expecting someone to be the dad you decided they should bem sets you up for pain"

Start to notice what you expect of other people so you can begin to see where some of your pain comes from.

It is not fair to expect people to live up to the imaginary person you have made up in your head.

Meaning Making

The other thing that really hurts us is the **meaning** we give things. Years ago I went to a Landmark workshop and they told us that we are meaning making machines. Life itself has no meaning, except the meaning we give it. We have the choice to choose what life means.

For example, he cheated which means he never loved me, and I am going to be lonely forever.

> *"How About, He Cheated Because He Was Horny And Entitled And Not Mature Enough For A Monogamous Relationship"*

How about, he cheated because his brain saw an attractive woman and she was open to the interaction and he was not able to control his primitive behavior.

How about, he has decided you don't love him and he wants to feel wanted and needed so is using sex to fill his loneliness.

I am not excusing the behavior for the man. You do when you stay with him. I am simply showing other meanings. Remember, understanding without boundaries leads to a life of regrets and wishing.

We are in control of what we have made everything mean. Once we realise this, we can start to step back from making everything mean something and allow the space of learning.

Expectations

One definition for an expectation is a "strong belief that something will happen." This means we are trying to control the future or predict it. Another definition would be when we have a strong belief that someone will do, act or achieve something.

"Love Does Not Hurt, Expectations Do"

When this doesn't happen the way we have decided it should, we then roll out the thoughts and emotions, leading us to a behavior and hey presto, more mess.

Play Off

Here are some examples and how the thoughts can play out inside out heads.

Expectation: I expect that he will spoil me on my birthday and make everything all about me, he will be home early and spend copious amounts of money on me.
Meaning making: If he does not, this must mean he does not love me. If he is late home, it must mean he does not care about me and never loved me.
Recurring Thoughts: He never loved me. He doesn't love me.
Pay Off: I don't have to get vulnerable with him and work on my unrealistic expectations in our relationship. It can be his fault; I will be right. I like being right. I am, therefore, better than him, because he is wrong.
Emotion: Sadness. Anger. Resentment. Jealousy. Fear
Behavior: Ask him if he's ever loved me and if he is cheating on me. Cancel dinner plans and cry in the room. Decide all birthdays suck.
Result: Relationship is being damaged.

Another example:

Expectation: I expect him to show up to all his child's sports days and pay child support on time.
Meaning Making: If he does not, he doesn't love our child and it's because he is a useless dad. He is a bad person and is too busy making his new family and has just walked out and left me to raise the children alone. This hurts me because how could you not love our child, the most amazing creature on the planet. What an arsehole.
Recurring Thought: He never loved me. He doesn't love me.
Pay Off: It can be his fault; I will be right. I like being right. I am, therefore, better than him, because he is wrong. I won't have to work on my wounds. I won't have to take responsibility.

Emotion: I feel bad for my child now. It is so sad that he doesn't love him. I hate him. Pity. Sadness. Anger. Hatred. Resentment. Jealousy.

Behavior: Message him he is a low-level scum sucking dirt bag and that the kids don't care. Add to it that they are hurting, and everything is his fault. Tell the kids dad doesn't care and we can't afford Christmas because Dad doesn't care. Also tell him he's not welcome here. Threaten him with custody and tell him his new gf is a dog.

Result: Everyone is hurting.

"He's Not Fucked In The Head, He's Just Not Doing What You Agree With"

The Pause

When we have been in survival mode for quite some time, we bypass the pause.

There is no time to pause when we are being hunted down by a grizzly bear, or beaten by a partner, assaulted, person or screamed at by a parent. We learnt we needed to survive, and in survival if you pause, you die.

What we need to accept now, is that we are safe. We can breathe now.

"I AM Safe"

It is now time to practice the pause. When you feel your adrenaline rise into your chest, which for me is the feeling of emotions taking over, go straight into your 5 senses and the breathe. Observe yourself, what do you notice? What are the thoughts? Where is your breath?

Learn to go straight into this observation mode and to not react. Practice by using the 5 senses to bring yourself back into your body. Ask yourself:

> What can I touch and touch 3 things? (Take them)
> What can I smell? (Take a sniff)
> What can I hear? (Listen to them)
> What can I see? (Notice them)

Once you have done this do your box breathing, inhale for the count of 4, hold the breath for the count of 4, and exhale for the count of 4, hold for 4. Repeat this breath 4 times.

Now ask yourself:

"Who Do I Need To Be Right Now To Get The Best Result For Myself And My Family?"

Remember your future self you met at the start? How would she be showing up? What was her guidance to you?

Make Time To Write

"There Is A Reason People In History Have Written"

Most of the people around the world who have a calming presence, who seem to be able to tackle the big stuff without faltering, journal.

You see social media articles telling you to journal, but you say, how? How do I journal? What do I write?

Journaling is a process. I will share with you a couple of things it does. One is a creative process, the other a logical process.

This process allows us to get to our upstairs brain and combine our left and right brains which makes use of all the parts of our brains.

Upstairs brain: Controls empathy, reasoning, decision making, morals, values and play. This brain is called the *cerebral* cortex. It's the brain that makes us look at our children and think, oh wow what a considerate child. It is the think before you act brain. This brain is not fully developed until our late 20's.

Downstairs brain: Responsible for reacting to emotions, freezing and flight activation and breathing. It is the act before you think brain and its job is to get our basic needs met for survival. This brain is called the *amygdala* and is what makes us look at our child and say they are having a tantrum. When this brain is in use it takes over the rest of the brain. It literally shuts down our ability to reason. We have no use of the upstairs, left or right brain.

The **left brain** is our logical brain, the **right brain** is our creative brain. The left is facts and the right brain comprehends. Some call this masculine and feminine.

Getting all the thoughts onto paper allows us to feel heard. Once we feel heard we can then bring logic which is the left brain into the equation. Then we go to the upstairs brain and use our values and empathetic skills. After that we can jump to the right brain and grab some creativity to come up with solutions and finally, we connect the left and upstairs brains together to decide what action we must take.

Reason number 2:

Journaling moves all the logic, words and our knowing's from inside our brains and puts it onto paper. It brings it into the physical which makes space inside our brains. With that new space the magical part of us, our higher wisdom, flows through and out our hands onto the paper. Some people call this channelling, I call it freaking awesome! We will often find that we now journal new messages, ideas, epiphanies and understandings.

"It Is A Way To Receive Guidance From Ourselves, To Ourselves, For Ourselves"

Here's some ideas to try out

1. Have a glass of water to sip on as you go because water is flow.
2. Start with as little as 5-10 minutes and leave the phone off.
3. To prompt yourself start with a sentence such as:

Lately, I've been thinking a lot about...
Last night I dreamt that...
Parenting is feeling really...
I'm worried about...
I've been fantasising a lot about...
During sex I feel like...
I feel the happiest when...
This relationship....
My family...
I'm unsure what to do about...
I wish I...
The thing I dislike the most about myself is:
The reason I do not succeed is because I am:

Tell me how I can:
To be happier I need to:
The thing I hate most about my body is:
When I look at happy couples I feel:
Growing up my dad treated me like:
When I think about my mum I think:

4- Make this a private journal or burn as you go.
5- Do not proofread your journal

Journaling is a free flow process with no parameters. If it turns into forgiveness, let it. If it turns into a "fuck you" letter, let it. If you get messages from your guides, and soul and ego, write them. Do not filter the writing. It is what it is.

"It Is Yourself That You Are Hiding From"

Sneaky Thoughts

Let's take a snapshot of what is being said to you, inside your own mind. Figure out what the payoff is. Later we will take this and find a healthier way to get the pay off.

Thought *Payoff*

Unbecoming Thoughts

"You Have Fat, You Are Not 'Fat'"

A lot of our thoughts are things we have been told and have taken as a fact. Go into a disempowering thought you constantly have and answer the below questions.

With the story you have made it, we need to learn to separate from it. Realise it is just the story, it is not us. To break this thought becoming our behavior, we can use humor, music and visualization.

For example, I had a story that I was so difficult which means that no one can help me and everyone gets annoyed at all my questions. This meant that I was showing up in life quite stand offish and difficult. At one of the retreats I attended in Bali I was assigned the tune happy birthday (on my actual birthday). I sung the words 'I'm so difficult" in the happy birthday tune. This takes away the power from the words and lightens it up.

What is the thought you keep having?

Who first told you that and when?

What is the attached story?

What can you name this story?

What tune will you attach to this story?

Meaning Making

This work requires you to be honest and truthful. Often times when we are honest, trigger an emotion that has been stored deep inside our bodies for a long time. Do not be surprised if you feel pain ad aches in your body, or suddenly have a stomach cramps or headaches. The emotion needs to released. Let yourself let it out. Remind yourself that this is temporary, just a passing phase. This too shall pass. (That phase made me want to cry just now. I would not have survived without that belief. This too, shall pass.)

Outline the facts of what was happening when you were triggered:

What have you made it mean about yourself?

When did you decide this?

What is the lesson from this?

Beliefs

Sex, such a wonderful act isn't it? Or is it? Some people believe sex is dirty and so is their vagina. Some people will believe blowjobs in alleyways are an act of love and to keep a man you must do all the things he wants. Some people will believe that sex is the most magical wonderful experience and have it every day and get paid for it. Beliefs are not facts. They are what shapes your world and you have full control over them.

Sex is:

My vagina is:

A pussy is:

Fucking is:

Making love is:

Sex is best with:

Sex is great when:

If you sleep with more than .... amount of people you are:

How important is sex?

Is it ok to have sex on the first date?

If a man pays for dinner should you give him sex?

If you don't give a man sex he will think:

Beliefs

To understand beliefs, take one of your beliefs that is disempowering you and write it below.

My beliefs about sex are:

Because of these beliefs I act:

I choose to replace these beliefs with:

Meaning Making

How have you come to the conclusions you have come to? Are you deciding that one man is the same as all others? Are you listening to well-meaning but uneducated friends? Have you concluded that there is only one way to do a task? Is it working?

Outline the facts of what was happening when you were triggered:

What have I made it mean about yourself?

What have I made it mean about the other person?

What am I making it mean about my life?

Where else is this showing up in my life?

What is my ideal outcome?

Who do I need to be to achieve this outcome?

Sneaky Thoughts

What are the persistent unhelpful thoughts you are saying?

Thought   *Payoff*

Unbecoming Thoughts

When we say we are we are fat over and over, our brains look to make it become reality. 'I AM' affirmations are so powerful. Helpful or not, the brain believes what you say and gets to work to prove it to be true.

What is the thought?

Where did this thought come from?

What is the attached story?

What can I name this story?

What tune will I attach to this story?

Meaning Making

Life means only what we make it mean. Even if you do not have a faith or religion consider the fact that if we choose to believe in magic, life feels better. If we choose to believe we have no choices and we do as we are told, life feels bitter. Do you agree?

What are the facts about the situation that triggered you?

What parts have you made assumptions about?

What are you making it mean?

What is the payoff for this thought?

What is this teaching you?

What can you do to that is helpful?

Beliefs

A belief is something that you say over and over in your mind until you decide it to be fact. It doesn't make it a fact. If you believe that money is the cause of evil, it will be all your brain looks for. We look for proof. If you believe that money brings freedom to be kind. You will see people being kind with money. Program your mind accordingly. First see what beliefs you were pre-programed with.

Money is:

People with money are:

If I had a lot of money I would feel:

Poor people are:

My parents told me that money was:

I am able to earn:

I am comfortable with ………… amount of money

I deserve money because:

Beliefs

Look at one of your money beliefs and ask yourself how it is showing up in your bank account.

The disempowering belief is:

I say to myself that when it comes to money I AM:

The most disgusting thing I think about myself is that I am:

Because of this belief I act:

I am now choosing to believe:

The new belief will allow me to behave in this way:

Sneaky Thoughts

What are the persistent unhelpful thoughts you are saying?

Thought	Payoff

Unbecoming Thoughts

What is the thought, what is the story you have made up and how can you diffuse it?

What is the thought?

How old were you when you first thought it?

How does this show up in your life now?

Picture the thought as a character and name it:

What does this character want?

What song tune will you attach to the character to diffuse?

Meaning Making

If you have not already read Don Miguel's book, The Four Agreements, I highly suggest you do. This book is a full philosophy for life and parenting.

I was triggered by:

The facts are:

The story I made up is:

I have made this all mean:

I first felt this feeling when:

Am I willing to let go of the meaning?

The value that can assist me right now is:

The 'I Am" affirmation that I will focus on this week is:

To work through this past wound I will:

Expectations

Write down what expectations do you have on other people? Answer the questions and then decide which expectations are helpful and fair, and which ones are not.

What am I expecting from my most recent partner?

What am I expecting from my child's parent?

What expectations do you need to let go of?

How will you let go of them?

What is the new intention you have for your relationships with the above mentioned people?

Expectations

Write down what expectations do you have on other people? Answer the questions and then decide which expectations are helpful and fair, and which ones are not.

What expectations do you have on yourself?

What expectations do you have of your children?

What expectations are you forcing on your children based on your own insecurities? (P.s: This is called domestication and is common. Allow any mum guilt that arises now to be noticed and remember it only matters how you move forward and become better.

What are these expectations hiding?

What is my ideal outcome with my children?

What is my new intention:

Beliefs

Betrayal really kicks us. It makes us feel that we cannot trust. Yet, if we look deeper there is always a meaning attached. For this exercise look at beliefs so you can find freedom in creating new ways of supporting yourself and trusting people.

The disempowering belief I have is: I believe

The thoughts I think inside my head because of this belief are:

Because of those thoughts I behave like:

I realise the belief disempowers me because:

This is my new belief:

Beliefs

The great thing about beliefs is that once you realise they are not helpful and they are based on old data, you can instantly update, change, delete & wipe them out. They don't need extra work. Poof. Gone.

People who cheat are:

Cheating means that:

If I cheated it would be because:

The percentage of unfaithful men in the world is .... %

People who stay with cheaters are:

Solo parents are:

Broken families are:

If you leave the father of your child that makes you:

Divorce is:

Marriage is:

Divorced solo mums are:

Divorced solo dads are:

Meaning Making

Radical responsibility is when we decide that everything in our lives is an effect of what we have participated in. It takes 2 to tango. It takes 2 hands to make a clap. You are 1 half of the equation, always. Be responsible for you 50%. If you react you will make a clap. If you do not, no clap will be made. Thinking in this way means that we have the ability to make our lives better and we are not bound by someone else.

What are you noticing about yourself and the meanings you make?

What are you noticing about the responses in your body?

What are you doing for yourself to allow yourself to let go of past hurts?

How can you parent yourself through your pain? What would you do if your child was in this situation?

Are you taking responsibility or are you trying to blame externally? Blame never works, it means we cannot change the way we feel. Responsibility means we can recreate our world.

autumn

PART: BREATHE OUT

"I Can See Clearly Now, The Pain Is Gone"

"Do Not Fear

going into the pain,
be only afraid of
the pain going into
you"

True Colors In Autumn

"If Seeing Is Believing, We Better Know What We See"

Isn't autumn beautiful. Come and sit outside with me and watch the children play in the crunching leaves. Look around at the photographers taking photos while the leaves are golden. Isn't nature beautiful when she is letting go?

Earlier in the book I mentioned the 4 pillars to stabalise our homes. The second pillar is clarity, the ability to see clearly. Please take the wool from your eyes now so that you can live with eyes wide open. Yes, you will see things you do not want to see but you will also see beauty that you never knew existed. Clarity is yours for the taking.

We went through winter so that we could begin to see what is working for us, and what is not. So that we could heal a little bit from our world changing around us and learn how to trust and allow the support of other people.

When we remove what was blocking the light, we see what we once could not see.

"Confused Minds Make Confused Decisions"

You can choose to process things gently and with compassion. The universe is giving you only what you can cope with.

Think of the rose bush that gets pruned right back to bare minimum. It feels counter intuitive to prune something so much, yet every season the rose bush blooms better than it did the year before. Instead of thinking about to do lists, or tasks, think of pruning off the dead branches to allow your energy to go into the fresh branches.

Personally, I find this season the most exciting season because I know it is the most rewarding. It is the season of epiphanies.

"The Truth Is The Truth Weather You Admit It Or Not"

Letting Go vs Purging

"If Seeing Is Believing, We Better Know What We See"

As with the rose bush, too much weak, twiggy growth compromises bloom. Suckers and sprouts can take over if they are left to their own devices, weeds can strangle the plant all together and if another plant is planted too close and shadows the rose, no one will ever see the magnificent flowers. Do not prune during a frost, which in our case, is winter.

"Pruning Spurs More Growth"

Sometimes we do not know that we need pruning. We can not see any blooms, or any growth. The best place to start with this is to start. Everything in this book is designed to show you where you need either let go, nurture or create.

"Basics, We Go Back To Basics"

Journal. This habit highlights to us where we have habits & unhelpful thoughts. Being aware means, we can now redirect ourselves when we find ourselves speaking or being in a way that takes up space with negativity.

Make space. This is the un-closed tasks that you have still hanging around in your head. Big ones and small ones. It's the things like, hang the washing out. Bake a cake with the kids. Get your hoo hoo waxed. Cut your babies toenails. Take the car to the mechanic for a checkup. Ring the lawyers. Get the tooth fixed. Leave your fuckboi. All un-closed loops are taking up space inside our brains, keeping us hanging onto the past and stopping us from moving forward

Declutter the home. The Marie Kondo method is now a trend. This process of removing all things that do not bring joy to the touch, is a process of purging. It clears space energetically and physically. Feng Shui works on all levels. Get the book "The magical Art Of Tidying Up" and start the process of decluttering.

Weed the garden. Clear the rubbish bins. Empty the car out. Put the washing away. Clean the fridge out. Feng Shui moves energy around. It takes the stale energy and leaves space for new movement.

Move your body. Yoga, walks, jogs, boxing, swim, dance, it doesn't matter. Just move your body, it shakes up the stale energies.

Cleanse. Cleansing is necessary when you are full of shit that isn't helpful. Once you are at a normal level your body will take care of all the cleansing. Think of this as the full mechanical service rather than just the oil change. Drink lots of water. Do a veggie only juice cleanse. Buy a cleanse. Drink lemon water. Do a cleanse.

"The New Does Not Want To Share Space With The Old. Out With The Old"

Journaling - Take Two

Here are some further ideas around writing.

Compelling Reasons To Journal:

1 – A problem shared is a problem halved. Through expressing all our issues unfiltered, uncensored and without judgement onto piece of paper we feel heard. We have allowed ourselves freedom of truth. There is no risk of consequence, judgement or rejection. We can now see the mess for what it is.

2 – Gentle emotions now have room to show up. Here is where we start to hear what it is we are really missing and thus, searching for.

3 – Moving something from your mind, through our hands is one way to get into your heart. Now that we have an idea of what we are looking for we get to begin to answer questions. Such as, what sort of career would make me happy? What sort of characteristics do I desire in a partner? We activate our logical brains.

4 – Planning happens. Now that we have an idea of what it is, we desire in life, we can begin to make small habits that move us closer to living that sort of life. We now have the capacity and the calm about us to make the plans.

Continual journaling removes the gunk as it is made and keep us coming back into our hearts. This is what allows us to manifest our best lives.

"It Always Looks Different On Paper"

I am going to share with you an excerpt from my journal.

The clarity I received from the days journaling; was a clear idea about my judgements towards myself, how confused I really was and what my true concerns were.

From there I moved into forgiveness work, in particular I used the forgiveness wheel and forgave a layer from every area of my life.

Here goes, its messy, its raw and it worked!

Online Journal Entry

>Oh gosh I don't even know where to start, it's like well, where was the beginning. I also don't want to do this. I would rather keep procrastinating and telling myself why i suck for not journaling. I don't usually blame the universe for all the things, but I want to blame something right now. Not in a dis-empowering way, but more in a seeking to understand why and how it's all come at me from every angle possible right now. And for the records universe, NO MORE. I GET IT. Ok. I am doing the 'work."I am writing this stuff.
>Ok so i suppose i should just write. and see what comes out. fuck spelling, fuck grammar and fuck making sense. yeah so ********* said my posts were full of swear words. Now i am noticing i am trying not to swear so much. maybe he is right. maybe i am a fowl mouthed little shit head. i am embarrassing him. this morning i thought about his mates and how they are not liking anything anymore and i made it mean they are all talking about how horrible i am. i am inconsiderate and rude and it is personal. i think they should quit taking it all personally i am, ffs. This is my life. but, maybe i am wrong.
>
>CONCERN: am i a fowl mouthed potty mouthed embarrassment?

I notice every time I swear now, i want to say sorry. I am unsure if this is helpful or not helpful. If people swear ALOT in a dictating way, I don't like it much. But I never take it personally. Well maybe it triggers me because its dictating and i feel like i can be too bossy.

CONCERN: am i too dictating and bossy. Look at my resting bitch face.

Is it my responsibility to fluff what I am saying so that it is not hurting my family? Or is this hurt around their ego and not even about being considerate?

Notice what came up for you whilst reading my journaling. Did you judge me? What did you make it mean about me? Did any of it trigger you? Did you want to be kind and sympathetic to me? Notice what happens inside your mind. Write it below.

I noticed that I thought:

"You Can Not Lead Anyone Else If You Are Not Leading Yourself"

Who Will You Be?

"To Be Or Not To Be, That Is The Question"

It's time to update your daily habits. Who will you be now? For each of the below, write the one thing you will become. *E.g.: For my mind I am practicing observing my thoughts. For my emotions I am learning more about anger.*

→*For my mind **I AM**:*

→*For my emotions **I AM**:*

→*For my body **I AM**:*

→*For my soul **I AM**:*

Making Space - Energy

Some energy in motion feel light and some feel heavy. The heavy emotions feel dark. Keeping secrets, doing things against our moral system or values, doing things that are opposite to our lives purpose slowly kill our soul. Our light starts to dim. The truth is that the real pain comes from us going against our own intuition.

What keeps you awake at night?

What emotion is attached to the sleepless night?

What are you not prepared to admit to other people?

What would your value and moral system have you do?

Use the next page to right down the moral dilemmas you need to align with your values and vision.

Closing Loops - Energy

What do you need to close off, so that you are aligned with your values and morals? Note the task in the left column and the due date in the right.

	Due

Expectations

Write down what expectations you have on other people. Once you have written them, decide which ones are helpful and fair for your ideal relationships.

What expectations do you have on your work colleagues?

What expectations do you have on society?

Making Space

Letting go is beautiful when done at the right timing. When we hold on excessively, letting go feels impossible and it turns into a full purging process. Learn to let go when you first feel the nudge, rather than to wait until you are forced to let go. Your dream life cannot manifest when there is no room for it. Simple.

What is taking up the most room inside your head?

What is stopping you from closing this off?

What resources do you need and how can you find them?

What 3 things can you do this week to get this ball rolling?

Closing Loops - Alignment

You are the one who must live and die with your choices. Write down what things you must reconcile in your mind. Which value/s this aligns with next to it.

	Value

Sneaky Thoughts

List the recurring thought/s that trigger you into an emotion that feels horrible. What is the payoff from this thought? What is it costing you?

Thought	Payoff	Cost

Unbecoming Thoughts

Use this sheet when you are feeling triggered. What is the thought, what is the story and how can you diffuse it?

What is the thought?

How often do you think it?

What is the attached story?

Picture the thought as a character and name it:

What does this character want?

What song tune will you attach to the character to diffuse?

Making Space – Children

Sometimes our children irritate us to the point we want them away from us. A great deal of times this is due to them needing connection, other times it is simply because they have picked up energy from other beings that you do not align with. Teach them spiritual hygiene and clear them every day.

Are you in your own energy? (you will get a clear YES, or a no or something in-between. If it is not a clear yes, it is a no.)

Is 'insert child's name' in their own energy?

Now what I would like you to do is ask the universe to put you in your own energy. It's simple. "Archangel Michael please put myself and my household members in our own energy. Clear all attachments and energy that is not serving our higher good. Do it now and do it gently." If it is possible, close your eyes while this is happening. If you have sage, palo-santo, a beach and things of that nature please use them. Clear the people, then clear the home. Remember to clear the car too.

How can you make spiritual hygiene a daily habit?

How can you learn to clear energy, ground your energy and then protect it? How about the children's?

Expectations

Write down what expectations you have on other people. Once you have written them, decide which ones are helpful and fair for your ideal relationships.

What expectations do you have on your partners children?

What expectations do you have your partner about his children?

Making Space

The universe needs space to land great ideas. If you are full of commitments, thoughts, heaviness and worry, it won't matter what the universe sends you, it won't land.

What is the most worrying thought that rattles around inside your mind?

What conclusion have you given the future?

Do you know this to be a fact?

If this is true, what can you do to best prepare yourself?

How can you shift your energy towards it, so that you can act in faith and support of yourself?

Use the next page to list the loops that you need to close regarding this matter. Start with doing 3 a day.

Closing Loops

Just like seasons, for our best growth, we must let go, close out, clean up and move on. List everything that you know needs to happen to close this out. Put a 1 next to it for top priority and a 3 next to it for a lower priority.

	Priority

Making Space - Body

Our bodies carry stale energy because old emotions and wounds are embedded inside us, causing us niggles and pain. We ignore it until it is so bad that we can't move. Where else in life do you do this? Notice the pains inside your body and start looking at how you can get these loops closed off.

What is the biggest niggle or pain in your body?

What is stopping you from closing it off?

What resources do you need and how can you find them?

What 3 things can you do this week to get this ball rolling?

Ask the universe to send you the right people to assist you with clearing the energy from your body. Research into Louise Hay's.

Closing Loops - Body

No health, no life. No feet, no walking. Write down the pains inside your body and next to each write what Louise Hay says about each thing. Start healing each body part.

Ache	Louise Hay Meaning

Making Space - Environment

A large percentage of the space that is taken up inside our heads, relates to household tasks as simple as putting the rubbish out or changing a lightbulb. Look deeper into these tasks and how they could mirror you. If you have a garage full of old rubbish, it would likely mean you have a stored in your mind and body a lot of old rubbish. If you store other people's junk in the attic, it would represent you store other people's junk in your head. If you constantly clean the surface benches but never clean behind the fridge, it would likely represent that you only heal surface level issues. Start to notice the connections. The inner world manifests in the outer world, alchemy. Cleaning up and making space externally is the doing part of the be do relationship. Your outer world reflects the inner world. Look for the clues to show you where you get to do deeper work.

What is taking up the most room around the house, that you have been wanting to sort out?

How does this make you feel about your ability as a person?

How do you feel when people come to your home?

How do you feel about mess in the house?

How do you feel about unwashed dishes?

How would you feel to have all your tasks closed off?

How can you get this closed off and cleaned up? List your action plan below:

Making Space - Image

I have spent an extraordinary amount of time hating what I see physically in the mirror. Thoughts that may rattle around your mind about your body are serious space wasters. Look at my nose, my nose is ugly, omg my nose, look at it, squeeze it, poke it, hate it…for fuck sakes woman! Find a way to focus on the beautiful things you see in the mirror. If you first notice what you do not like when you look at yourself, you will be teaching the children to do the same. First, identity the thoughts, second either improve it or find a way to accept it. Finally, magnify what you do like.

What do I think about myself when I look in the mirror?

Of the things above, what can I do to improve upon each one?

What resources do you need and how can you find them?

Of the things that cannot be improved upon, how can you accept them as they are?

What do you love about yourself when you look in the mirror?

Ask the universe to send you the right person to assist you with clearing the energy from the body part. Research into Louise Hay's work around the body.

Beliefs

Beliefs can be quite tricky. It is not until we look inside that we even realise what beliefs we have. Our values keep us stable and safe so make sure that you have done your groundwork. Let go of beliefs that do not serve you and replace it with something that does.

Example: I believed all men cheat. Therefore, I would allow cheating in my relationships and brush it under the table. It caused me to feel insecure and crazy. Once I realised that was hogs wash, I chose to adopt the new belief that boys cheat, men don't and there are plenty of men in the world.

List your beliefs around men:

List your beliefs around females:

Beliefs

To understand beliefs, take one of your beliefs that is disempowering you and write it below.

What is the disempowering belief

What do you say to yourself

Describe how it shows up in your behavior

How is it disempowering you?

What is the new belief?

PART: BREATHE IN

"In The Dawn I Rise...

And what A
Magnificent
    Dawn It Is!

"I would never

have settled for
a lifetime of
'sorrys'"

Create & Connect

"Intuitively Manifest Your Life Now"

Welcome to spring, what a time to be alive you guys! It is sunny outside. The air is crisp. The baby birds are singing in the morning light, the light pink buds are fragile on the fruit trees, the morning is dewy and the newborn lambs are trying to stand.

Springtime is that of birth. It is the time of connection. Connect yourself to nature, to the universe, to beautiful souls, to dreams and to your heart. You deserve to feel this moment so stop for a moment and connect.

Springtime energy is the hearts energy, it is the essence of vitality. The birthing of the new. The creeping in of the morning light after a long cool night.

If you have arrived here after autumn, you will be fresh with new ideas and energy. This is an exciting mood, everything around you looks great and you feel confident, creative, intuitive and grateful.

This is the time when the mornings feel energetic. Spring energy doesn't need every new bud to become a full-grown flower. It just simply enjoys having buds and has no expectations on the flowers or fruit.

"The Beauty Is In The Moment Not In The Outcome"

Dream, get clear on what you truly desire and manifest it, start doing daily rituals, spiritual hygiene, yoga, vision boards - all the things to connect with the creator and of course, the girl in the mirror.

Start writing that book, start the program, learn the stuff, launch the idea baby girl! Let your inner child out to create some magic in your life.

This is the 3rd pillar to your stable home and you guys, its sunny outside.

"Do Not Give Your Heart Away Again, People Do Not Need Two Hearts "

Intuitive Creation

There are numerous ways to hear what is being presented to you by the universe. What is important is that you find a way for you to channel your own messages.

I love using pastels and a large piece of paper. I set the space with music and incorporate nature, elements and my senses. So something nice to smell, touch, see, hear and maybe taste.

You can involve the children in this later down the track. To begin with, they are quite distracting. I do absolutely encourage you to show the children how to intuitively create. Just allow them space and keep it super simple for them.

I recall the first time I really tuned into doing this. It was one of my first nights on my own, after our separation, because my ex had our daughter. When we were together I could count on 1 hand the amount of times he had her and I did my own thing. It was an amazing experience and I remember going into this different state and being so aligned to the random music shuffle. My message was

"I AM STANDING UP"

Eminems song, "I'm Not Afraid" became quite a strength for me to call on. I never know what I am drawing. There is no logic or thinking. I put pastel to paper and allow whatever is to eventuate, to eventuate.

From there I will pull some cards and align it with the drawing. Usually there are messages to record on the drawing, and it explains what I have drawn. I just listen to what I am hearing inside my head. Sounds nuts doesn't it.

> *"You know what though, even if it is nuts, I am content and happy and is that not what life is all about?"*

That's the thing with faith, all that matters is that it is guiding you to a better place. Next time you are looking for a movie to watch, watch Eat Love Pray. It's such a good movie.

After I have finished drawing, I pull the intentions for the month from the drawing and cards and make a list of them to place on the fridge. I then have a very clear months focus. The intentions always start with 'I AM'.

This is how I intuitively create what is coming, what lessons and layers I will be working on and a basic overview of what to look for along the way. I have plenty of these videos with me doing it, on Instagram. Feel free to go and check it out.

Whatever you do, find a way to record your guidance from an energy that is creative and non-judgmental. Oh, and colorful.

I run intuitive creation workshops at my home in Hamilton, New Zealand. If you would like one at your home contact me for pricing and numbers.

I Am In My Own Energy

If you are an empath, you will sense other people's emotions, sometimes to the point that you may not know where theirs starts and yours ends. This can make life challenging. It is draining to work in your purpose when you are feeling everyone else's emotions.

Imagine there are invisible spiders everywhere and when you are not protected they can jump onto you and start weaving a web between you and their owner. This allows the spider to travel back and forth between the two of you, or a lot of people, and mix the energies. Yuck!

Be spiritually hygienic please. I teach spiritual hygiene 101, which is the basics of clearing yourself, cutting chords, grounding and protecting your energy.

Here are some crucial questions to ask:

1. Who does this energy belong to?
2. Can you return this energy to source now please?
3. Are my roots deep enough and strong enough?
4. Is my aura too close, too far or, just right?
5. What color energy does my aura need to be filled with right now?
6. Am I in my energy?
7. Is this energy serving me?

Imagine it is like cleaning a toilet in your home. As you can imagine, there are a lot of different people that crap into that toilet. If you don't clean it bugs fester and soon, it would smell so bad you wouldn't want to go near it.

Clean your auric field more than you clean your toilet. Energy travels way faster than toilet bugs. If you carry fowl energy from a lifetime of thugs, I'd have to put on an entire suit before I came near you. If you want better people in your life, clean yourself.

"I Am Aware Of Other Peoples Energy"

Feeding Your Self

"Exchange Energy, Never Power"

Learning to fulfill ourselves is the best tool for self-love.

We look to others to fill in voids, the holes, the past hurts. In doing this we are giving them the power to control what we 'eat', how we eat it, when we eat. We gave them our power which is also known as 'disempowering'. To become empowered, we must power ourselves.

One of the reasons separating is excruciating is because we have made the other person feed us. Who will feed us now? Will we now starve to death?

This is a co-dependent behavior and this is something we must work to change within ourselves before we couple again with another. Unless of course, we wish to repeat the pattern.

I hear people disapproving of other people for the power games they play, it makes me think of all the time I've played with power. I mean be honest, power feels really freaking good!

Empowering ourselves means that we won't need to, or want to, take power from other people. Notice the people who do play power games and observe how they are using it as a means of fulfillment. Please do not say anything, just observe to learn. Remember, people mirror our lessons to us so if you are seeing things repeatedly in another's behavior, it is showing you where you get to go to work in your own behavior.

If you have given your power away, I would like you to close your eyes and quiet your body. Practice the box breathing for a few minutes. Put your hand on your heart so you can focus on being led by your heart.

Now go up to the people who have your power and ask them very politely and with assertion to give it back. Hold your hand out and take the power back. Thank them and notice the light in them. Put your power back where it belongs and remind yourself that you can love another with all your heart, but you are **never** to give you heart away again.

Feeding Your Self

"It Was Not Love At First Sight"

Use these sheets when you notice that you are suddenly playing into a game of power. This is quite often a text argument where you feel you simply must have the last say. Interactions that have you reacting and feeling hot headed.

What is your real problem?

What is the pay off, what is it feeding you?

What is it costing you?

How can you feed yourself?

Bitchs' Got The Pimp Juice Too

"Sex Is Not Love, Love Is Love"

For centuries women have used the power of the pussy to manipulate men into succumbing to their wills. And called it healthy. Joked about it. Praised it up. Sung songs about it. Laughed about it. I know. I'm one of these women.

How is it we have allowed ourselves to justify our behaviour our power plays and then we condemn men for reacting with their cocks.

We love seducing men and then wonder how 3rd parties enter the bedroom yet it's all about power and filling voids.

Woman love to pussy whip a man. The more he throws away for her, the more power she feels. The more he hunts her, the higher up she feels. Have you ever watched the movie "The Other Boleyn Woman"? It's a great movie, worth a watch.

Power plays are power plays. I've shown you the effects of having no boundaries in a relationship, and the effects of having no boundaries as a single woman is becoming the home wrecker. It's bittersweet when I say, both are forgivable because both are signs of a woman in pain and lacking self-worth.

Ladies, if you absolutely must wield the power of your pussy over men then at least do it with single men. When you know what you are worth you will not take a man who is being unfaithful. It is not a sign of love for him to cheat on his partner with you. It is a sign of a man who does not have boundaries and lacks assertion. I have never yet heard a good excuse for a man to cheat on his wife. Not the kids, not the business, not her mental help.

Empowering ourselves comes from internal worth and self-love. Knowing that we are here for a reason. Taking responsibility starts with looking at where and how we get our power, where and how we manipulate and where we pretend, we don't.

I have had plenty of interactions whilst being single with men in relationships and there were times that I wanted to forget my boundaries and do the do. What stops me, is literally, the girl in the mirror. I take myself to the mirror in the bathroom and I look into my own eyes and ask myself, who are you being April? Who does your future husband require you to be? Hot Italian willing to cheat on his wife is fun sure, (in my head anyway, sometimes reality is different), but what does that make you?

I know better, I do better. It is a conscious choice. To know, is not enough. The other thing that stops me is knowing that in the future I do not want to feel insecure in a relationship because I know how easy it is to be with a married man. I want to believe that women like me are taking over the world. Woman who I can trust. It all starts with us. Stop making a mess.

I am saying:

1. Power lies in the heart not the pussy
2. Look at how you use sex in your history
3. Figure out what you have made sex mean
4. Exchange energy not power
5. Don't have sex with men in relationships

I once read that addictions are things that create problems in your everyday life. If sex makes problems in your everyday life, then I would consider that to be an addiction. Russel Brand has an amazing book called Overcoming Addictions, I used this to start to break my sex addiction.

Also, consider the idea that you are addicted to the relationship. Co-dependency is also, in my perspective, an addiction.

" It's Not A Skill To Have Magic Cooch"

The song by Charlie Puth, Attention, sums up this behavior quite well. You just want attention. With children I would say it is not attention seeking, it is connection seeking. The same can be said of you.

Feeding Your Self

Power games are not easy to recognize when you are feeling weak. Instead of focusing on why he is doing what he is doing, focus on what keeps you allowing it? What do you need to heal?

What made you feel that you simply must react?

What keeps you going back for more?

What is your pay off from this situation?

What happens inside your body?

When did you pick up this pattern?

How can you be more confident?

Girl In The Mirror Music

"It Was Not Love At First Sight"

The beauty of asking questions is that you are accessing consciousness. You are asking the unknown to provide you with insight and awareness. When you ask the questions and allow space, the answer will appear.

After one of my very first coaching sessions my coach asked me "How can you learn to feed that to yourself?" I just tell you now, coaching wasn't comfortable for me, yet I enjoyed our sessions because I knew I would grow. So, if you feel uncomfortable with the emotions that arise after realisations, just know it is part of it. To know the light, we must know the night. Right?

I don't know was my initial reaction. I sat with that question. How can I feed myself?

At the time I was making bath salts. I noticed when I did this I was completely out of my head. I wasn't in pain and ideas would flow through. The same would happen when I would paint furniture and garden.

"Creativity Is Meditation"

It allows our minds to go still with the noise, and it makes space for the ideas to flow in.

I started to write little notes with little quotes and ideas.

One evening I was feeling a bit gloomy when a love song came on and thought to myself (notice I captured the thought), "I wish someone would sing me love songs, I miss it."

The next morning, I wrote "Sing love songs to yourself April!"

I Got A Vision Of A Room Full Of People Singing Into Hairbrushes Against A Side Wall Of Mirrors.

The next day Addison started to play her newest favouritist song "The Girl In The Mirror" sung by Sophia Grace, feat Silento. I felt that feeling inside my body, the feeling I would soon come to know as my inner self telling my physical self 'YES."

And so, we began to sing it together in the mirror. To each other, to ourselves and then to Instagram. It was terrifying for me to put a video of me singing in a mirror on Instagram, which is exactly why I did it. Fuck it. Post.

"This Process Taught Me To Feel The Cringe And Do It Anyway"

It taught me to sing love songs to myself like I meant it, to move my body and feel the energy of my own love, to look into my eyes and see myself, how to be confident.

It gave me strength to show the things I was embarrassed about on a social forum. Once I realised that I could do it behind the screen, I looked for how I could become the same person offline as I was online.

Quite judging your process. Life is the process. Don't you get it? If you are evolving, you will be in a process. Accept it.

I have music playlists now based around my healing. I suggest you do the same. Here is a few of my favorite love songs that I sing to myself.

> Take it easy – Stan Walker
> Truly Madly Deeply - Savage Garden
> No one – Alicia Keys
> I'll Be There – Jessie Glynne

Also – find or create the song that aligns with you biggest WHY. Mine is Whitney Houston "Greatest Love Of All." I've known this for around 5 years. I just knew. Again, I had been asking what my purpose was and this song came on and it fucked me up. Tears, heart swells...all the emotional reactions. Our bodies react to what they know to be true. They provide information. Whakarongo. (Listen.)

And remember, every other woman that your ex is with or been with, is inconsequential to your life's mission. Your purpose couldn't give a flying fuck about her. Catch up baby girl.

Girl In The Mirror - Lyrics

I wake up every day like hello, beautiful
'Cause this world is so crazy and it can bring you down
You're too short, too fat, too skinny
Hey, well excuse me if I think that I'm pretty
So I don't care what you say 'cause I'm original
I'm learning how to love me from my head down to my toes
Let 'em know, let 'em know if you with me
Hey, 'cause I finally found the answer is in me
My mama she keeps saying
Don't let 'em get you down
Had to learn to love me
That's why I'm talking to the girl in the mirror
Like even if you're down, better get up
'Cause every set back's just a set up
For something just a little bit better
Oh, I'm talking to the girl in the mirror
Girl in the mirror, girl in the mirror, girl in the mirror
Girl in the mirror, girl in the mirror
Go to sleep at night with a smile on my face
'Cause I know who I am, and I can't ever be replaced
So go ahead, be proud, be different
Hey, just make sure you're one out of a million
So bae you did it, you took it to the top
You gotta keep going, the grind never stops
Say you won't do what I won't do
Yeah girl, I'm watching you
You got that swagger, you got that glow
For all the doubters, just let them know
Count up more, for days just go
I love your soul and your rhythm flow
Like oh yeah, I'm like oh yeah
Put your hands in the air
That girl power, that girl power
Put your hands up for the girl power
I like it, I won't bite it
Keep it on 'cause I'm watching
Keep going, just kill it
So girl embrace your number one chance

Girl In The Mirror lyrics © Warner Chappell Music, Inc, Kobalt Music Publishing Ltd., Sony/ATV Music Publishing LLC

"Happiness Is Not The Goal, Peace Is"

Feeding Your Self

Part of our journey from self-hate to self-love is self-acceptance. An area plenty of woman struggle with is assertiveness and boundaries. The issue is we think if we don't bend over backwards for everyone else, no one will want or love us. It doesn't matter, because if we don't love or accept ourselves life will continue to feel like something is missing. That thing that is missing, is the connection to ourselves.

Being assertive allows us to implement healthy habits and routines that prevent us from getting stressed out, angry or overwhelmed. Anger as an emotion arises when something crosses our boundary. Usually this is because we have been passive. Empathetic parenting is based around being assertive and having an emotional intelligence around your emotions. What does anger mean to you?

How do you deal with your anger? Do you allow it in a healthy manner? How can you work with your anger in a healthy way?

How can you implement healthy habits around the home so that you have less reason to feel guilty at night?

What is anger?

What is hatred?

What is love?

Feeding Your Self

Start to notice how you set your life up to gain approval and likes from other people. Is your home clean for you, or for the world? Do you give a guy a blowjob so that he will think you are amazing, or is it from truly desiring him? How much of what you do is to gain attention and approval?

How do you respond to male attention?

Do you dress for yourself?

Who are you trying to impress, and what would that feed you?

Who do you desire to be for men?

Daily Habits

It's the small changes, bit by bit, that make the lasting feel good behaviors. Look at your negotiable habits and your non negotiables. These are things like clearing the table, making the bed, teeth brushing, manners and the likes. Do this for the entire household.

What are non-negotiable habits in the home for you and your family?

How can you encourage everyone to keep to them?

What is the reason they are non-negotiable?

Are these reasons reasonable? If so, write these up on display and have yourself and the family focus on keeping to them. Make it fun.

Feeding Your Self

Spiritual hygiene 101 is as important as your daily shower. If you are not having a shower every day, start now. Make you bed every day and make it a goal to keep one other surface in your house tidy and clean every night. I would like you to learn how to ground, clear and bubble your energy, the homes energy and your children's. Also, learn how to put an aura cleaner at your front door. Rituals and routines are as much fun as you make them! I love doing the witchy things!

Are you and the household in your own energies?

If not, how can you get into your own energies?

What spiritual hygiene habit can you implement on the daily?

How can you calm your mind and center your breathing on the daily?

How can you practice being mindful of your energy?

"Seek And Ye Shall Find"

summer

PART: UNCONDITIONAL
"Look Ma, I Am Standing"

*And What A Stand
It Was.*

"Show The Way
as you go the way"

Empowered Action

"We Can't See The Sun Rise With The Curtains Closed"

Summer is here, can you smell the BBQ and sunblock? All year long we have been looking forward to the months of summer and now she is here you better make the most of it!

We can hear the festival music, we wake to the kids laughing and playing on the trampolines, we here the kids arguing while splashing in the water, we get prickles in our feet and search for our lost jandles and we feel good!

Eat the fruit, pick the flowers, stay awake longer and soak up the vitamin D. There is not much to say about summer because in summer we are empowered. Empowered people know what the fuck to do, who the fuck they are and the get it the fuck done!

Listen though, if you have more than you need, please give some of it away. That is the beauty of the path. I did it, I showed you. Now you show someone else. Just never get too focused on them that you forget that your cup must always be full first. Your cup then the children and then the wider world.

Take the time to notice how far you have come. Notice that you prayed for this desperately in winter.

"You Didn't Think You Could Get Here. And Yet, Here We Are"

You will notice by now how much more connected to who you are, you are. You will by now have let go of people, places and emotions and find yourself with new people, places and emotions.

You will know that you cannot stay in summer for too long, you will lose your appreciation and growth if you do. You are well and truly on the path and complacency is not an option. You will continue to grow, to lead.

Summer is about energetic aligned action. It is a time of being empowered. It is associated with our legs, our support system. The power we have within us to move wherever it is we choose.

Empowerment is the 4th pillar to your home. You now have the ability to get SUPPORT, to gain CLARITY, to CONNECT and to be EMPOWERED. This is everything you need to be stable and build your dream life on. As long as you keep these 4 fundamental lessons in practice, your home will be stable.

You have already chosen the direction of your dream and now is the time to spread the light. Go and meet new people and collect smiles.

Remember to appreciate yourself, your creator and this journey.

"Create That Project, The Universe Will Meet You Halfway"

Daily Habits

I love when I get a moment to tell you what to do! Honestly, I can be quite bossy, opinionated and dictating. It is such a practice for me to allow people to be who they are and live life their way. It's a practice for me to accept people are on their own paths, at their own times and that my way is not the only way. If I can do this, so can you!

TASKS TO COMPLETE OVER THE NEXT 30 DAYS

Visit a yoga class and complete a full class between now and 14 days.
Journal your birth story.
For 10 days in a row wake up drink a glass of water, meditate for a minimum of 10 minutes and then move your body for a minimum of 10 minutes. On completion look in the mirror and thank yourself for choosing yourself.
Listen to James Clears audio book ' Atomic Habits"
How much water can you commit to drinking for the next 10 days?
What exercise can you commit to for the next 10 days?
What meditation can you commit to? (One giant mind app is great)
At the end of 14 days come back and journal here what you learnt about yourself

Feeding Your Self

It is up to you to ask the universe to respond to you and provide solutions. Ask the universe to show you the way and thank her when you notice how she is. Ask to be shown compassion, love and sunlight. She will show it to you, you must notice it and appreciate it. The universe wants you to feel love. Real love. Not conditional love.

What do you need support with right now?

How can the universe support you?

How will you notice the universe responding?

What 'I AM' statements can you affirm to yourself in the mirror this week?

What are you appreciating about yourself right now? Name 3 things.

Daily Habits

Small tiny things can make huge differences. Start to work on small daily habits that take you closer to your vision and strengthen your values.

What is a great song that makes you feel empowered?

What is a 5-minute daily habit you can implement that empowers you?

How can you make this habit stick? Do you need to change your routine around? Find extra money? What? And how can you make it happen?

What takes most of your time?

Who Will You Be?

Who will you be now? Who do you desire to be? What will you be like? How will you show up? How will you feel? For each of the below, write the one thing you will become. *E.g.: For my mind I am practicing observing my thoughts. For my emotions I am learning more about anger.*

E.G.: I am meditating 3 times a week.

→ *For my mind I AM:*

→ *For my emotions I AM:*

→ *For my body I AM:*

→ *For my soul I AM:*

"No Is Enough"

learners

PART: EMBODY

"Because Somebody Calls Me Mum"

*And What A Wonderful
Call It Is.*

"Your Voice Becomes

your child's inner voice.
Feed your child a voice so
 certain, that no one would
 ever dare cage her
freedom"

ww.consciousfamilydynamics.com

The Children Are The Future

"Your Children Require You To Have Confidence"

Our children right now are growing up in the 'See me, hear me, understand me,' generation.

You were raised in the 'seen not heard' generation. That generation taught you that it's not possible to have an equal relationship with your children and to raise good children you must be a dictator. Another words the common belief is that when an adult gives an order, a child must obey.

Have you listened to the lyrics of the song "The Living Years" sung by Mike and The Mechanics? Our parents are only teaching us what they believe to be correct. We are doing the same to our children. None of this work will stick if you continue to hold blame towards your parents. Remember if you wish for your children to allow you your imperfections, then you must live and breathe this first. Honestly, your parents could have aborted you. It's too late when we die.

"You Know Im Going To Be Just Like You"

The world needs more parents to stand up and stand for their children whilst being empathetic and raising decent human beings. The struggle *is* real. Too many parents are hiding in their homes wishing and hoping, scrolling Instagram while their homes slowly fall apart, their souls are slowly crushed, and their children unstable. Right?

Nothing real is stopping you from parenting with more love, more peace and freedom. You *can* wake up with energy and love for the school morning. You *can* be in a happy loving and trusting relationship with confident stable children. You have freedom to be yourself.

I couldn't find mums or families who set the example of the person I wanted to be. And yet here I am, living this life with confidence, being me.

The freedom to travel. The trust in myself. More acceptance in my role as a mum. More empathy. More patience, understanding, fun, intuition. Are these not the things that you desire to have?

Yes, you can have all these things, I am living this life right now. A life where I spend most my days feeling gratitude and love. Days full of connection with deep friendships. Feeling in love with my daughter and at peace co-parenting. Knowing that my daughter has more connection with both her parents now than she ever did before. Isn't that the goal?

Children need you to be yourself. When you know how to be confident within yourself as an empathetic parent you will turn up your intuition and be the key for changing the entire family's dynamics.

Another song that captures how our behavior creates the future is "Cats In The Cradle" by Harry Chaplin.

> *"My Child Arrived Just The Other Day, He Came To The World In The Usual Way; But There Were Planes To Catch And Bills To Pay"*

You will find that as you change you will to create, find hobbies and enjoy life again. You will play with your children & enjoy a laugh. You can learn to feel amazing naked, to dance in the mirror and begin to accept yourself. The dark, and the light.

People often underestimate the power of being ourselves and overestimate the power of being what others want us to be. The power is in the acceptance of our feelings and the consciousness to not behave through our emotions.

People still believe that authoritative "I'm the boss' parenting is the only way. That being the controller will bring peace and contentment? It never has. People believe that they have to live a hard-challenging.

"It's Just The Way The Cookie Crumbles, But Who Even Wants A Crumbled Cookie?"

We all want the same things. To feel empathy, intimacy, safety. To feel accepted and a belonging. We all want to run down the streets with our arms out retched, necks arched back roaring like a lion.

Practice natural parenting, yes, it is work but so is being grumpy. It is choosing to be conscious of what is going on when we are feeling triggered and not taking things personally. It is accepting that the way our children feel is part of being a human. It's natural to have feelings and someone must teach us how to be with them. It's a continuation of growth, trying new things and re-evaluation.

"It's A Committed Relationship With The Goal Of Being Connected"

Practice, It's A Practice. A Conscious Practice. Surround yourself with people who are always striving to be better.

Not perfect, just better.

As we turn to ourselves in the mirror, so too will thy neighbor.

"The People Of Our Land Will Begin Hold Up Their Own Cup; 1 By 1 They Will Rise"

My Guiding Principals

-Where I have a will, I have a way.

-My child(ren) are my legacy.

-Dream it, Believe it, Achieve it.

-Where the mind has been, where the mind has seen, the mind can go.

-The cup overflows or the well runs dry

-I don't know what I don't know.

-Always be open to discovery and learning

You would not run a business without a set of plans and structures, right? Well then how come you are trying to manage a home that way?

"I Am A Woman With A Mission To Bring Our People Home To Their Natural Style Of Parenting; Free From Worry & Judgements"

What Guides Your Whanau

What are your family values, guiding principles?

What are your family's current goals?

What does it mean to be family?

"If You Are Not Being You, Then Who Are You Being?"

Empathetic Parenting In Action

Step one in empathetic parenting is the paraphrase. This technique lets them know that we are listening, that we understand and that we can see them. Seeing is another way of saying that you are in the present with them. This action lets them know we accept them. We are not trying to change or correct their feeling. It is futile to try to do so anyway, the feeling has already happened, and it is trying to undo the past.

Emotions are Energy in Motion remember. Visualise them. See it inside your head. The word motion means it is happening right now, it is in the present. You cannot undo that. All we can do is allow it it's phase and learn how to use our emotions in a healthy manner. For children, this takes guidance and practice.

A word of caution stay away from judgmental dictatorship parents while you practice this. I left many places in tears because I went against my intuition and tried to 'shut her up' or stop a fight. I tried to make her play nice or say sorry when she wasn't. I always felt like complete and utter shit because it is against my principals to parent that way. Find other people to be around while you are building up your strength.

Paraphrasing is repeating the words someone says in questioning or accepting manner. Use the same words as if you were reflecting. If someone says this says that they are cold and you say to them, you are chilly, they would not really feel heard. No, I am cold...

If they say "This really sucks" repeat the word sucks! If they curse in an aggressive manner than that is likely a boundary that has been crossed. Usually it is an amygdala reaction. That requires a different approach and paraphrasing will not work. If you need extra support then contact me for coaching packages, I would love to teach you about the child's brain linked with generational patterns. It makes me fizz seeing people breaking patterns, like fuck yeah girl, that's ma gurl!

With the amygdala tantrum you would distract them. They think they are in danger. They need to be distracted so their brain can reopen the logical and reasoning sections and close down the fight or flight brain.

Paraphrasing can look something like this example below:

Outburst: This really sucks! I hate you!
Paraphrase: Wow, this really suckkkks for you? (empathise the sucks without adding aggression)
Outburst: YES! AND I REALLY HATE YOU! You are mean, you are not my friend! Meanie meanie meanie!
Heard: You really hate me right now, I'm a meanine mummy and you don't want to be my friend. (nod the head, soften your face. Tilt your head to the side etc. Make sure you are not sarcastic, they will know.)
Communicating: Yes Mum. I hate that you won't let me stay awake this is my favorite program and it's not fair, you are so mean right now.
Understand: Naw baby. You hate that I won't let you stay awake past your bedtime, to watch your favorite program tonight and it's not fair is it? (Add in a tiny bit of reason/logic. Keeping face soft and arms soft. Be soft so if they need to fling themselves into your arms they can. The sooner they melt, the better right?)
Truth: Yeah, well how come you get to stay awake longer than me? I don't want to go to bed by myself. (throws himself into your arms and cry's like it's the end of the world.)
Flex: Oh. Well honey. My body doesn't need as much sleep as yours and bedtime is bedtime, right? How about I sit with you and sing you a song tonight while you fall asleep? Would you like that? (soft and accepting. You are the safe place.)
Connecting: Oh yes, can you read me my favorite book about the red fire engine as well?
Seen: Yes if you quickly get there now we will have time. Hey honey...
Receptive: Yeah mummy?
Acknowledge: I'm really proud of how you let your feelings play out just now. Lets remember that bedtime is bedtime ok.

That was a perfect world example. Obviously, that is the aim though. Interactions that you can guide into accepting, diffusing and coming though whilst keeping boundaries means that in the future there will be less outburst.

Be aware it won't always be this smooth. Sometimes in our minds we will literally think "fuck this, do as your damn fucking told", or something equivalent to this. We struggle to parent empathetically when we are triggered in our owns lives. For example, if we had just received a really high power bill and a message about someone we dislike our emotions will not be calm and we would struggle to accept our child's needs on our energy.

This is why it is important to do all the other work concurrently. Empathetic parenting on its own will not work. Parenting techniques on their own do not last the distance of life. Assess yourself, what worked well, what needs to be refined?

Another way to deal with the same situation would be if he still wanted to stay up and we moved into the "yes, honey, however, in this home bedtime is 8pm." Its assertive and it acknowledges that he has a feeling and a want. It doesn't dismiss him. It then reinstates the boundary which is bedtime is 8pm. From here if the child continues to ignore the clear directive, we would offer them a 'cause and effect' option.

It is time to go to bed. You can either walk into your room and grab a book for us to read together right now, or I can carry you to your room and we will not have time for a book? Which will you choose? You must follow through on the second option. Do so calmly. Do not threaten with crap you won't stick to such as "I will take all your toys for a month.". Say what you mean and mean what you say.

The cause and effect technique works because it allows them to make a choice and feel some control. Start to practice. Either you do……Or you can…. Let's go and dive into joint parenting.

"Pushing Or Forcing Just Recreates The Past"

Yelling Trigger

We must get into the habit of asking ourselves what triggered the emotion. We can learn this by noticing our thoughts.

What triggered your yelling?

What was the pattern?

How can you interrupt that next time?

How Can I Connect

Your intuition with your children is second to none. No one knows more about your tamariki than you. You are given all the tools you needed at birth to fulfill your life's mission and guide them on theirs. Whatever has happened to this point, accept it as part of the plan. It is the most empowering perspective. From this point onwards, your job is to trust in your ability to know your child. This is my jam! This is what I'm all about, you can never convince me that connection is not the answer. It is the key to everything in parenting. Your intuition is the door, and connection is the key. Use these prompts to dial in on what you know of your children.

What are the children actually asking for from me?

What are our families non negotiables?

What are my children's current needs?

How can I meet them?

What is good about my parenting that I cannot see?

What program or course can I participate in to improve my parenting?

How can I listen to my children and allow them a safe space to express?

What do my children love most about me?

How can I connect with them?

"The World Needs More People To Stand For Freedom, Whilst Raising Human Beings."

Co-operative Parenting

Learning to co-operatively parent with someone takes time. Please understand that what you are doing is creating a new way of relating with the man who fathered your future. Your intention of what this will look like, will make all the difference.

Creating a new relationship with someone that you have had a child with is weird because you have to change the way you perceive them. You can no longer flirt with them, talk about your dreams, cry into their laps, speak about your pain and cook them dinner unless you have strong boundaries.

If you do not accept them as they are and accept the relationship is no longer a committed monogamous one, then you will struggle to be around them.

When you can openly speak to them with no intention of making them jealous, about any love interests you may have, that is when you know you have healed.

Promises that were made and not kept are now called betrayals, broken vows are called divorce, homes that were used to nurture our children in are now called houses, places that were frequented by you as a couple are now avoided, friends and family get divided up and divvied out, money is argued about and then there is the children and pets. Who gets what?

"A Lot Must Change. A Lot Must Die And A Lot Must Be Born"

Take a deep breath in and let a deep sign out whilst dropping your shoulders. Did you do it? Guys come on, I am the coach and you agreed to try on my suggestions. Breathing is part of living, breathe.

This word co-parenting usually is used once a couple separate. However, co-parenting is really something that ought to be impressed upon all parents irrespective of the relationship. It means to work together as a team towards an agreed goal.

Divorce is fucking shitty. It is brutal, it is heart wrenching and it is also liberating, sweet and loads of fun. I mean, ever heard the word cougar?

When we are experiencing upheaval in our lives and we feel the blame is on the person who did not keep the promises, it is easy to decide that their feelings do not matter, and since they fucked up, you will make all the parenting rules. After all, they are the one who left the family, not you.

Now if I had to be completely honest, which I do because I expect you to do the same, I would tell you that sometimes I still feel like he is the one that created this situation.

My pay off for this thinking is that I don't have to deal with sorting any new challenges that come up nor feel bad about how this may feel for him. It costs me freedom. It costs me creativity and it costs me connection. As long as I blame him, I don't have to change. I do not have to get any better.

> *"To Interrupt This Pattern I Look At My Daughters Little Face And I Smile At Her"*

I refuse to be incongruent. Now that's not to say that their aren't things that I do that do not fit 100% into my word or teachings, because let's face it, sometimes I have a laugh and do really immature things with my girlfriends because, well, I can. What I do mean though is that I put a time limit on my shadow side, and I face towards my intentions and best life vision.

As my coach would say to me over and over; "April, you can have your excuses, or you can have your results." I now repeat these words to you. You can have your story, your victim story, or you can have your results. Make a choice and then make a move.

This is an extract from the current legislation printed on the New Zealand's Ministry Of Justices website.

> (c) a child's care, development, and upbringing should be facilitated by ongoing consultation and co-operation between his or her parents, guardians, and any other person having a role in his or her care under a parenting or guardianship order:

It is exceedingly unhelpful to stay bitter, judgmental or hurt at the actions of your ex-partner, or to be fair, any person.

A lot of people get extraordinarily confused when it comes to what child support is. We all need money but in the most supportive way I can say it, check yourself before you wreck yourself! Child support is about supporting the child not about how much time someone is entitled to.

"A Child Is Not About Who Pays For It."

Please hear what I am saying. Your objections that you have about your money concerns are valid, you may have been left in the lurch with a lot of stress. It is very scary.

Hating on him will not change your situation. Find a way to support yourself. Work on your money story which is linked to self-worth.

"I Am Capable Of Supporting Myself."

If this is something you need to go into, use the money belief sheet. Your bank account is directly related to self-worth.

Learn to not rely on the child support. Notice resentments coming up, expectations, bitterness and do the work. Learn to accept people are where they are and that includes your ex who may be spending money on 'her' kids. It hurts I get it; I honestly do. Especially if he is fathering a new child and seems to not have time or money for your child. It hurts because of what you have made it mean. What have you made it mean?

If you can't seem to move past this and you find yourself telling the children mean things about him and how he doesn't care, please get in contact with me to organize some coaching sessions to take you deeper through this work.

If you have plenty of money, you may find that instead of hating on your ex for not giving you money, you get mad that he isn't spending time with his child. It all boils down to the same thing, what you have made it mean and a lack of accepting that he too has his wounds. Get on your path.

At the height of our separation I wrote a tell all blog about my ex-husbands mistress. I was so full of rage to the point I was riddled with fever. I had a respiratory infection, a bladder infection, kidney infection and a fever. Inside my body I had so much hatred and defiance towards him and what I dubbed his "unapologetic mistress."

I had gotten to the point that I was so affected by her constant slandering of me on social media, and him still acting like it was acceptable and treating myself and Addison differently when he was with her, that I realised I had to stop all communication with him.

To this day I do not understand how she made me out to be the one in the wrong. The difference is that now, I understand that we are completely different people driven by different motives in life. Hurt people hurt people. I no longer am triggered by her existence because I no longer have to face any shadow work relating to her. I went deep as fuck with it because I knew if I did not, I would not be able to be the mum my child needed me to be.

"I Had To Lead Our Family. I Had To Go Through The Dark And Get To The Light"

I knew that if I did not, our lives would not change.

"Who do you need to **be** April?" my coach Emile asked me. "A fucking bitch." I replied.

And I was, for a day or two. I was all sorts of nasty. I said things that I would never say in a million years. For the first time since knowing this man, I wanted him to hurt. I sat on the plane bound for Bali and sent him messages designed to hurt him. I wanted him to feel what I felt, and to know I blamed him for everything. I was disgusted in him and my simultaneously.

I despised him and I was fed up with being disrespected by him and her. I was fed up with being left to parent on my own. I had no space to perceive him as an individual person who was entitled live his life and do things that I didn't agree with. Because I was still playing wifey, I was still being the person I was in our marriage…judgmental.

"A really good mum. That's who I need to be."

Once I allowed myself to drop my pride and hatred and know what it was, I needed, I instantly started to become it. This was a defining moment for me because I realised if I was to be anything, it had to be that. From that moment on everything I did was centered around the question of "is this what a good mum would do?" I have not stopped being this way.

So, to backtrack a tiny bit, when I arrived home from Bali much had changed. More agreements had been broken and it was hammer time. The house was now on the market & the custody journey though family court began.

I was up and down. I'd be racing around at 3am refusing to sleep and waking in the morning just to have to run outside to dry retch on the frosty winters grass.

And all the while I healed and I learnt and I cried and I mum-lifed and Ihoe-lifed and crashed my car and I freaked out and I wrote and I dreamt about better days.

I invested in my healing as a priority because that is what I believe good mums do.

At the start of cutting contact and erecting my boundaries, our daughter became bedridden with a fever. For 5 days and nights she did not get out of bed unless she had to go to the toilet or to the doctors. When she did get out of bed on day 6, I said something about her father, she cried and went back to bed with her head hung low. She was depressed. My 7-year-old was depressed.

"I Needed To Separate Myself From His Emotions"

The thing is, she had no idea when this would end or even if it would. She was feeling her pain, my pain and his pain. She was in deep emotional turmoil.

I just knew who I had chosen to 'BE' was a 'good mum.' I knew that this was a part of us rewiring our dynamic and the more work I did, the faster I could get to supporting her in healing. I knew I could not do it without my own healing.

In hindsight, I see that she walked with us. She fell when we fell, she ran when we ran, breathed when we breathed and now, she has dropped into a beautiful energy, because we have. If her internal base is grounded than the external doesn't affect her as much. Meaning, if her father and I are grounded than she will be able to ride the waves of external life.

I remember moving to a bigger house so I would have space to have private phone conversations away from Addison's ears and I thought that was good enough. Yet she could still feel the energy, she could feel my bitterness towards him still.

Children are tuned in to both of you. Please realise it is self-absorbed to think you are the only one that matters to your child. Even if he did the worst of the worst, the child still feels for their parent. Feels sad, sorry, anger...something.

You only have to look at all the grown arse adults around you who hold resentments, judgements, pity and regrets towards their parents to see that what I am saying is the truth.

"It Is Our Job To Release Ours Pain So That We Can Show Our Children How To Release Theirs"

If you are in NZ, I would encourage you to participate in a Plunket run program called 'Parenting Through Separation." It is a free program; you do not need a referral. Plunket speak to empathetic parenting also and it has made a profound difference in the lives of many. I also know in Australia there is something similar.

Never underestimate the power of a 3rd party teaching you and your ex how to parent after separation.

Also, while we are on the topic, do not assume your ex isn't in his own pain. Men feel a lot during divorce. Studies show men generally never recover from divorce and a lot of men still do not seek support, except for in the bed of another female. It is naive of us to think that men move on quickly just because they rebound.

"Hurt People Hurt People"

Find a way to accept that this is their journey too and allow them to their process, as you expect to be allowed yours. Remember that they have their story around what is happening just as you have yours. Truth is subjective.

As for the bed of another female, recognise when you are being this other female too. Do you allow yourself to be with men who are in emotional pain? Because if you do, know that this man is blocking your dream man.

"Give Up The Boy Crack"

Having crazy sex with passionate men can be addictive. Dive deeper into what it is about this energy that turns you on. I recently learnt that my body has its own mind when it recognises men in emotional pain. I was attracted to it. What do you fall for?

You do not need this sort of energy in your life to become who you are becoming. There are plenty of men where you are going. Sometimes we need the distraction or the detour to learn a few lessons, just don't stay with the detour guy. Rise in love.

Being alone to begin with is scary. A lot of woman don't want to share custody because it would leave a gap in their lives. That doesn't make it acceptable to use them. Notice if you are using the kids to fill the void and avoid the pain. Notice if you run a 'busy' story so you have no space to feel the hurt. Notice everything external you do to fill voids and work to find the way to feed yourself internally.

"Define A New Way. What Do You Want It To Look Like?"

If there is another female on the scene, let that be his thing. Don't make it your thing. Stepparents come and they go. There will never be another biological mum or dad. I do not mean disrespect to stepparents either. I grew up with a stepmother she will always be my parent. She well and truly earnt that right.

I simply mean, don't get into arguments or let her consume your thoughts. She is not the parent; you are not in a relationship with her and it is your choice on how you view how to be a good mum. Remember, hurt people hurt people and a woman who is trying to assert herself over you and your children, is a woman in pain. Do not engage.

Co-operative parenting is the goal. It is always the goal; it has never not been the goal.

I stand for those who are in the dark and guide them to walk towards themselves; so that they can become better parents!

Families are not broken just because they are not living under the same roof. That is a belief someone made up and spread out into the world. Pffft on that.

"My Family Is Not Broken"

Beliefs - Parenting

Our beliefs can free us or keep us stuck. Let's look and see what your beliefs are. Once you have noted them down, ask yourself if these beliefs make your life better?

I believe that good dads:

To be a good mum you must:

Beliefs - Parenting

To understand beliefs, take one of your beliefs that disempower you and write it below.

The disempowering belief I have is- I believe

The thoughts I think inside my head because of this belief are:

Because of those thoughts I act like:

I now see the belief disempowers me by:

I now choose to replace that belief with:

Children's Thoughts

If you could see the unspoken words behind a child's eyes, you may very well see the below:

-My biggest fear is being abandoned by either of you, I need you both.
-I don't like the way you stop me from seeing my dad.
-I feel like I am betraying you both and that feeling leaves me in a state of despair.
-I love both my parents and nothing they do changes that.
- Your opinion of my Dad affects how I feel about how he feels about me, which makes me decide that I am the problem.
-I'm sorry you are hurting, it hurts me that you are hurting, but it hurts me when dads hurting too.
-I hurt for all of us and I'm too little to know how to process this.
-I don't have hope or faith yet, I don't know how or when this is going to get better.
- I need you to make this structured for me.
-I'm scared to say how I feel in case it upsets you
-The more you fight, the more I hurt.
- I hate this limbo you make me live in.
-I need to know when I will see them next, if it isn't certain, don't get my hopes up.
-Get support please. I need you to be stable for me. I can't be the parent.
-I don't want to be a visitor. I want to belong in both houses.
-Please get up. Please laugh. Please come back to me.
-I don't know what I am and am not allowed to repeat so how about if I'm not allowed to know it, don't let me hear it.
-Please let me adjust before trying to make me love the new person and/or the new kids.
-My world just fell apart, not just yours.

"During The Times Of Chaos, Our Biggest Gift In Parenting Is The Connection With Our Children"

When we are connecting with them, seeing into them, feeling them, we are actually understanding their words without them speaking. When our children feel valued, our lives change for the better. Suddenly, everything gets better.

Heart-based action leads us to a better life. The longer we remain in ego-based decision making, the longer we are harming ourselves and our children.

"Being Really Well Behaved During Turmoil Is A Sign Of A Child In Need"

(e) a child should continue to have a relationship with both of his or her parents, and that a child's relationship with his or her family group, whānau, hapū, or iwi should be preserved and strengthened extract from: Section 5: replaced, on 31 March 2014, by section 4 of the Care of Children Amendment Act (No 2) 2013 (2013 No 74).

Tips To Move Ego To Heart

1. Go to a parenting through separation specialist at the first signs of separation.

2. Seek support from a coach.

3. Make agreements about parenting with yourself when you are in a heart spaced mood, hold yourself accountable to it.

4. Put yourself in your child's shoes as a reminder that this is not easy for them either.

5. If there are safety concerns and you cannot agree to a solution, seek professional support.

6. If speaking with friends is your way of coping, ensure you can do this out of earshot of your child.

7. Make your bed every day.

8. Set up a structure for your children so they can see, in advance, when they will see the other parent. If the other party does not have structured times but wishes to be involved, seek support to have this enforced sooner rather than later.

9. If you are already involved with another party, keep that as adult business until your child has grieved and transitioned to 2 separate homes.

10. Don't argue about money. Take what's offered and find another way to top up your finances.

11. Journal your feelings about the other parent so you can seek to create space to allow peace to enter your thoughts.

12. Remind yourself of the fact the other party loves your child. Remember the love they gave them and focus on that rather than the things they are not doing now.

13. Never cut the other parent off permanently. Always leave a seat at the parenting table for them.

14. Create a morning ritual with your child, even if its 2 minutes and 1 thing. It creates connection.

15. Cuddle, be affectionate with your children so when you don't have the words to say, you have the touch.

16. Practice empathetic parenting.

Perfect Parenting

How often do you feel pressured by society to be a perfect parent? Do you feel like you are being judged on the daily by 'better' parents? How often do you, be honest here, judge other parents?

Am I a perfect parent? No. Do I swear? Fuck yes. Do I yell sometimes and not listen? Yes. Do I sometimes sleep in and buy an artificial lunch on the way to school? Yes. Shit I even sometimes still feed my kid on noodles for dinner. Am I late to assembly's? Do I spend too much time on my phone? Do I get frustrated and wish there was an off switch on her voice box? Yes. So what. Shoot me.

You know who thinks I am perfect? My child. That little girl who smiles at me in the morning and says, 'good morning mummy." The girl who strokes my hair while I'm asleep. The girl who still wants to hold my hand down the street.

"Connect Before You Correct"

You know how I know that I'm doing a perfect job with her? Well, I quite simply observe.

> Me: OMG look at me I'm so fat I look so gross.
>
> Addison: Mummy!! You do not look fat and you are not fat.
>
> Me: Do you really mean that?
>
> Addison: Mama, it's what's inside (points to her heart), not what's on the outside, that matters. (Smiles at me and has doe like eyes).

It took 4 years to get pregnant and the second we conceived; I knew it. I remember saying 'We just made a baby." Of course, I felt stupid but inside I knew it. The second time we conceived I said the exact same thing only when I took the pregnancy test, I cried because I knew that it would not become earth side. Intuition is a real thing. Accept your weird knowing's. I feel my daughter and it took a lot of work for me to not confuse her energy withy my energy.

One day she was at school and I got a sudden urge to go and get her. I felt what I called anxiety and it was yuck. I started to drive to school and got stuck in roadworks and I remember feeling like getting out of the car and running. It was a stupid thought because school was still a good 15-minute drive away on a country road.

As I neared the school my anxious feeling peaked and I could barely contain myself when I saw police passing me. I knew they were going to the school. As I turned into the school road, I could feel my heart beating in my ears.

I saw the cops at the school, I saw one of the teachers directing traffic. I did not see Addison in her usual spot. I wanted to leave my car and run into the school and find her.

I stared at the woman directing traffic and watched as she recognised me and did not change expression. That let me know that she wasn't concerned about me because Addison was fine.

Anyway, long story short everyone was fine, and it was a simple car crash. Except, Addison had freaked herself out. On the drive home she shared with me her thoughts and her chain reaction to the crash that she heard from her room. I went over my chain reaction and was able to match my feelings to her feelings. Because I had messaged a friend, I had the time log and in hindsight, I was just feeling her.

My ego loves how intuitively connected I am. It is something I have been working towards for years. Yet how can I function at my ultimate levels if I am feeling my family and allowing it to overtake my senses? I am aware of other people's energies.

Let's go into some tips for being a confident mother.

.

1: This child was created from your flesh and blood.

Nobody else has a clue about what's inside them as well as you do, mothers' instinct is a real thing and it was a gift from god. It is your instruction manual. Use it. Close your eyes, focus on your breathing and if it doesn't feel right, it isn't.

2. Your voice will become your child's inner voice.

Get down onto their level and look them straight in the eye. Feel straight from your heart (trick is to not cry) and tell them how they make your heart feel. How the way they jumped in the puddle today, although you yelled at the time, makes you proud of them because you secretly admire their freedom and lack of inhibitions. How when they shared the toy with the baby at the mall, it made you want to cry because you love how generous and kind they are. Tell them good things every single day without fail.

3. Bath time, book time, bedtime.

This makes a huge difference. It's sometimes the only time we put our phones away and listen to our children, they will start talking to you about their little lives. Let them choose the books they like. No correcting when they are reading. It's about connection not education. Read to them books that express to them how much you adore them, books that teach them morals and values and books that are plain fun.

4. Parent Empathetically

When they are behaving in a way that is not acceptable to yourself, first acknowledge how they feel then set the boundary. This does not mean you allow them to be spoilt brats. It just means you have allowed them to have a feeling and then redirected them.

5. Apologise

Apologise to them. You fuck up, all the time I'm sure of it. If you didn't, you wouldn't be a human. Say sorry. Not when you're an emotional mess but when you are in the right frame.

Quietly look them in the eye and say I'm sorry for....." Show them what a sincere apology looks like.

6. Let it go.
Stop focusing on what you did wrong and focus on doing better. Focus on what you did right. Focus on loving yourself more today than you did yesterday. Once we learn to love ourselves, our little monkeys will learn to love themselves even more. This is self-love and monkey see, monkey do.

7. Is there any reason why?
Ask this question when you're pissed off at them. The answer might surprise you. Always seek to understand. Nobody wants a know it all because know it all's miss important things and are dismissive.

8. Let them fall asleep with you sometimes.
This one's simple. You know how you feel when you are lonely in the bed and just want a cuddle? Well come on now, kids love falling asleep with the one they love too, let them sometimes.

9. Remember their age.
This world is so fast paced that we tend to think our children are older than they are, they aren't. Their emotional intelligence is still being fostered. Acknowledge this and step back. In a world full of adults, we need our kids to be kids.

10. Laugh.
Be a dick with them. Dance and sing karaoke styles, show them the big kid inside of you. Let your barriers down with them. If your child doesn't tell you 'your funny mama', then you my dear have let life become far too serious. Take off the masks. Who are you trying to impress anyway?

Even just implementing one of these tips into your relationship with your child will make a difference.

Resenting The Children

Mum life includes every spectrum of emotion possible.

It's no lie that most mums want to, at some stage, strangle their kid, throw them out the window, leave them behind, smack them around the head or walk out the front door to never return again.

What happens with that energy? The resentments, the anger, the sadness, the guilt. All those vibrational feelings. Where does it go?

"It Goes Into The Relationships Dynamics"

The other thing to notice is when we are objectifying another person. Objectifying is when we make a person a thing and dehumanizing them. We lack empathy to things, and this is how cycles of abuse are born.

Thing – Arsehole. Ex. Bitch. Cunt. Dog. Slut. Chair.

The best thing you can do to stay connected is to call the person by their name or by something endearing. Even calling them kid, child and the likes, weakens the connection to them. When you are mad, learn to bring the human back into the picture.

On the next page I will give you an exercise to release resentments.

Release Resentments Activity

This is something the whole family can participate in. Make sure you consider each person's ability and age. So, for example, an 8-year-old who can read and write well and enjoys it may be able to do this for 5 minutes and write a whole page. A 10-year-old who dislikes writing and struggles at school may be able to do 1 prompt, 1 sentence and that is perfect.

You will all need pen and paper and privacy to write.

Here's some prompts.

> 1- I'm still mad at you for....
> 2- I wish that she would...
> 3- I feel...
> 4- I hate how...

Don't share the words that are written down. Don't peek at your children's work. Burn the papers. During the burning and the writing process be quiet, just be in your own space.

After you have released and burnt the heavier things, get a new piece of paper so you can write the new intentions.

> 1- I would love us to...
> 2- When I am mad, I will choose to...
> 3- I love how...
> 4- my ideal dynamic looks like....
> 5- I am grateful for...

You can ask each of your family member to read these out loud. Do not pressure other members of your family but do encourage and inspire.

A fantastic way to end this activity is with some movement. How do you as a family like to move? It may be a walk to the river, it may be bouncing on a trampoline, kicking a ball around or having a kani kani.

Dear Mama

Dear Mum,

I know you want it to stop. Just for a day. Just for one f*****g day I hear you tell your girlfriends. I know.

I don't do this because I'm a feral little shit. I don't do this because I hate you. I don't. I do this because I am still learning. I don't always know what to do.

I know you cry when you have yelled or treated me horribly. I know you get riddled with a heaviness that consumes your chest. I know sometimes you think you can't be a mum anymore & you feel that you are failing.

I feel it. When you want me to go away, I feel so alone, I feel scared that I am going to be sent away because I know I was horrible today. I know I am being selfish. Self-absorbed. I do not yet know how to let the feeling go when I am feeling mad.

I know you didn't get a rule book about how to do this thing with me. I am sorry. I am always sorry. Even if I refuse to say it. I promise I want to do better.

Mum, all I want is to feel loved. To be seen. To be heard. To be understood. To feel that who I am is good enough. That I have an opinion that's worthy of being listened to. That I am part of this family too, even though I am little.

I'm still young. I'm learning. Guide me mum. 1 moment at a time. Find us the support you need so you can be happy and confident. Show me what the boundaries are so I know not to mess with them.

Mummy, I believe in you. PS: I love you Mum. Xox

Be Courageous, Slay The Beasts

You are not a bad mum.

If you are a bad mum, that would mean your child is a bad child.

Because they are made from you.

You are not a bad mum.

These past few pages have had some really deeply infused energy. They may have you feeling all sorts of stink. Are you back in the woods now laying on the ground waiting for the beasts to feast on you?

> *"Slay The Beasts, Don't Let The Beasts Slay You!"*

The wound is the point in the body that the light may enter.

The fact that you have this book means you are wanting to become a better mum.

Do the work.

What is the purpose of guilt?

What is its message?

Where are you in the journey through the seasons right now?

What does this season require of you?

Do the work.

Guilt Gift

What is happening inside you when guilt shows up?

What have you made it mean about yourself?

How much progress have you already made?

What is good about this situation that you have not yet seen?

Bedtime Rituals

Did you know that the trick to running a smooth morning is to run a smooth evening? The morning starts the night before.

> *"What Do You Do To Mark The Ending Of The Day With The Children?"*

Think outside the box. What would work for your children and you? When my daughter was a baby, every night I would sing her twinkle twinkle little star with reinvented words. I bet you did something similar. What can you do now that works for your child's age?

So why introduce rituals?

    1 – When we add meaning to something such as a song, a smell, or a touch we anchor it inside our physiology and spirit. As parents, we can anchor these songs as moments of love with our children for them to remember later in life.

    2 – Rituals assist us in being more conscious with our children in the moment. We get to connect with them. We get to cuddle with them or sit with them at nighttime. Smile and or dance with them in the morning. Whatever we do, we are present in that moment with our child.

    3 – If you have more than one child rituals are a great way to bring the family together as one. You may call these family traditions?

    4 – When either of you hear this song it will instantly remind you of the moments you share, and release feel good endorphins.

6- Rituals shows our kids that they are important. That we cherish stolen moments with them. That they matter.

7- Rituals can mark the beginning of the day, and the end of the day in a fun and special way.

Fill Your Cup First

Visualise your children out in the hot summers heat, asking you to share the water in your cup with them. But actually, your cup is empty. When you go to pour, there is nothing but a slow drip.

Your child starts to cry from thirst. You frantically try to tell your child that crying will dehydrate them more, but the crying gets louder and more desperate. Their amygdala kicks in and they become uncontrollable.

Because your cup is empty, you are susceptible to taking on their energy as your own. You start to run around looking for water but you realise you are feeling so weak. Your legs aren't moving properly, it is hot. So, fucking hot. The nearest water well is at least a 10 minutes' walk away. Your ankle gives way.

You hobble to the well to gather the water to feed your thirst, to feed your child's thirst. When you get there, it is empty.

> *"The Well Is Dry. Your Well Is Dry. Your Cup Remains Empty"*

You sit down and you cry into the emptiness. 2 empty cups are laying broken beside you.

The cups represent your capacity to serve love. To nurture. To teach. The well represents your back up reserves of confidence, structures, routines, trust, support & friends.

And you, well you represent a mother who has not made time for herself. A person who is guiding another small creature on their walk on this earth but who forgot to invest in her own shoes and water bottle for the climb.

You must fill your well. You must fill your cup. So, when your child spills the contents of their cup you have reserves to serve them with.

You cannot serve from an empty cup. Do the work. Nurture yourself. Allow yourself "me" time. Allow yourself time with friends. Encourage yourself to get that haircut and write a poem. Let yourself sleep in. Put the structure at home in place. Do the work. Fill your cup. Say no to banging the ex's best mate. So no to blowjobs in alleyways. Say yes to coffee with people who uplift you. Say yes to boundaries around bedtime. Say yes to meditation or walks along the lake. Do the work.

"It Is Your Move. It Has Always Been Your Move"

My well is full. My cup is full. That is how I am able to not only support my daughter with her cup, but I am also able to show her how to fill her well.

Summer will come and when it comes, be ready for it. Do the work in the winter and autumn. Do the work in the spring and you will never look back.

Nature Elements

Living now is not the same as living in 1988. Our children don't spend the same amount of time outside; they don't spend as much time in natural water or stacking firewood.

They spend a huge amount of time around technology, stressed anxious parents and fast-moving energy.

"Just Maybe, We Need To Slow It All Down"

Here's some tips to grounding and calming ourselves and our children using the elements. I've also added in a few lines on each element, about how it influences us. Please look deeper into the element's influences.

Notice the shift in the children's energy and forget about any perceived mess, washing or work that may come as a result of taking on the suggested activities.

Just before you move to the next page, let's take a super quick look at how the elements work together for life and growth.

Let's look at how a tree photosynthesizes. If I was to relate that to humans I would say, let's look at how we can empower ourselves from within.

The roots from the tree absorb water and minerals so it can grow. It gets this from the earth that it is rooted in. (earth and water). The tree uses its leaves to breathe (air) and uses the light and warmth from the sun (fire).

If you wanted to release the elements we could start with the fallen tree.

If we put the wood from the tree into the bonfire, the water would evaporate from the heat, the light would shine out through the flames and the oxygen the tree has stored inside it from breathing would create energy and turn into ash. This ash would then return to the earth.

Earth Element –Supports Life

Practical, Hardworking, Mothering & Materialism

Earth is related to the winter times and is feminine in energy. This is the element for grounding and feeling like we belong. Because we do belong.

"Ashes To Ashes, Dust To Dust"

It gives us stability and strength through routine behavior. Connecting to mama earth is where we go to feel at home feel our connection to our physical bodies. It helps us to get out of our heads. (Her head is up in the clouds means; she needs to ground.) Earth supports our life, yet we must be the ones to plant the seeds.

Suggestion: Take your children to the river, the lake, a bush walk or even just a paddock. Talk about the nature that you see. Allow them to feel. Play some music if you like. Get them to walk barefoot or stand in the water.

Suggestion: Teach your children to ground into the earth by standing still with their eyes closed. Tell them to imagine that they are a tree and that colorful roots coming from the souls of their feet into the earth. Tell them that the roots can connect to a gorgeous crystal about half a meter below the earth. Ask them what color their crystal was.

In its negative expression, too much earth can lead us to being overly indulged with materialistic desires. If you have a lot of earth, you would need to bring some air into your life. Earthy people tend to focus a lot on the exterior and physical panes and forget about the internal worlds.

Everything is alchemy.

Water Element – Dissolves

Emotions, Flow, Loving, Intuition, Adaptation

Water is related to autumn and is a feminine energy. Water is nature and it flows. It satisfies thirst and it cleanses and purifies. It releases and represents emotions. It goes around obstacles and continues to flow. Without water we would not survive.

Suggestion: Baths are such an excellent source of cleansing and grounding. Place some Epson salt, rock salt, baking soda and essential oils into a warm bath. Try Lavender, Frankincense, Ylang Ylang, Sandalwood, Myrrh, Patchouli or other earthly plant type oils if they need to ground as well.

Suggestion: Allow your child to cry and say silly things or overexaggerated things for a moment. Tell them you understand. Tell them that it must be sore for them. Tell them you see how upset they are. Try not to fix the situation for the moment, just allow the emotions through. Once they have finished, hold them or cuddle with them. After a enough time, send them off to the shower to let the water cleanse them. Tell your child to imagine the water is washing away the yuck.

If you have too much water of the water element you may find you are sensitive and struggle to get practical habits that stick because water has no boundaries. You may also find that you have a hard exterior and don't like to let people in. Too much water and you may not ever bring to fruition your dreams, you require some masculine energy to make that happen.

What element can help with that?

Air Element –Fills Space

Talkative, Imaginative, Liberating

Air is related to Spring and takes on the masculine energy. Breath is the flow of life. The air moves things around, without it everything would become stale and die. Instead of saying the words 'breathe," breathe. Loudly breathe so that the children mimic your actions.

Suggestion: Teach your child to breathe if for 2 slow counts, hold for 2 counts and then breathe out for 2 slow counts. Basically, this is box breathing. Do it with them, place their hand on your tummy while you teach them. Then place their hand on their tummy so that they can connect with where the breath goes inside their bodies.

Suggestion: Head down to a windy area and run through the wind with your child. Let your hair blow in the breeze and breathe in the air whilst feeling the earth beneath your feet. Take deep breaths and ask mama nature to take away heavy energies on your out breath. Breath in freshness and breathe out what does not serve you.

Air has the ability to turn hot or cold without a moment's notice. It is affected by other people's boundaries. For example, if I shut all my doors up in my home on a hot day, I might arrive home to hot smelly air. The smell of food spreads through the air and it could be enticing or offensive. Air is much the same. In some ways you could say it is able to seduce easily.

If you have too much air you may find that you have your head up in the clouds too much and need to come back down to earth.

Fire Element – Fire Creates

Expressive, Warm, Inspirational and Passionate.

Fire is related to summer and is very masculine in energy. Fire is about passion, manifesting, action and making it happen. Fire lets nothing stop it and if you let it, it would burn all in its way. The sun provides vitamin D so remember to allow the sunlight on your skin.

Suggestion: Light a small candle at bedtime and play a meditation that incites imagination and manifesting magical journeys. Place red and orange colored crystals along the child's body whilst they fall asleep. Also use oil blends for calming, protection and intuition.

Suggestion: Do a visual manifesting dream/vibration board with your children. Use magazines, crayons, pastels & felts and teach them to close their thoughts off and draw whatever comes to mind. No analyzing and no pre-deciding what is to be drawn. This is the essence of intuitive creation.

Suggestion: Take your children to watch the sun wake up and the sun go to sleep. I find this such a magical adventure and over the winter I really miss my sun rises.

A side note on fire: It can also be destructive. It destroys buildings in a split second and kills people with its smog. If you use fire negatively you really can create a lot of mess. I was definitely in my fire energy when I wrote my blog to the 'unapologetic' mistress. In my mind I envisioned myself standing outside a house and throwing a grenade just to watch it burn the house down. It made me feel satisfied. That is the power of fire used in its destructive manner.

Do not mistake this destruction for true power?

What Is Your Element

I am a through and through Aries, full of fire, tenacity, destruction and creation. I gravitate towards other Aries and fire signs with Cancerian people coming in a fast second. Cancers are crabs which are water signs who are all about stability in the home. Naturally I know I need the water to keep me in creation. What is your sign and how does it show up in your life?

What element are you lacking and how can you find it?

Insincere Apologies

"Without The Correct Energy, Words Are Just Dots On Joined Together"

When we force an apology from people, we are saying something like this:

'Say sorry even if you don't mean it so you can satisfy my ego and allow me to feel right and make you wrong!"

Forcing apologies is teaching our children to say what they do not mean in the sake of politeness, diffusing emotions or really, making parents feel comfortable

I mean, what.

Imagine that little Johnny pulled Suzie's hair because Suzie kept trying to make him play with the barbie doll. Imagine Suzie was yelling at him and telling him that he must do what she says. Well Johnny got so frustrated that he pulled Suzies hair.

Johnny! Say sorry!

What the shit did we just teach Suzie? That its ok to try and force someone to do what they don't want to do, and then, they are made to say sorry because the way they reacted to the situation was physical?

Ideally Johnny's feelings about the control would need to be acknowledged, and Suzie's feelings about the hair pulling would need to be acknowledged. Next Suzie would need to apologise for her behavior, trying to make Johnny do what he did not want to do. Johnny would need to apologise for his behavior, pulling Suzie's hair. And then we could move to the logical task of where to from here.

Sounds easy huh. That's a joke, it is not easy! Some days I just want to yell FFS you guys! Quit it already! Some days I do yell that.

> *"It Doesn't Take A Rocket Scientist To See That Forcing Kids To Say What They Don't Mean, Can Take Them To Be The Adult Saying Sorry Just To Shut Their Wives Up."*

I will never force my child to say sorry for something they are not sorry about. I would rather teach her how her behavior affected someone else. Furthermore, I will never teach her to say sorry for how someone else feels, that would be saying that we have control on another's feelings. We do not.

So, let's teach by showing, the art of apologies about our behavior only. Never another's feelings.

Here's some ways I do encourage apologising for

> I am sorry for being rude.
> I am sorry for ignoring you.
> I am sorry for raising my voice towards you.
> I am sorry for not considering the effect on you.
> I am sorry for not speaking up assertively.
> I am sorry for betraying your confidence in me.
> I am sorry for throwing your toy.
> I am sorry for not having patience with you.
> I am sorry for not looking after your bike.
> I am sorry I did not keep my word.
> I am sorry I for trying to control you.

What Does It Mean

What does sorry mean to you?

Are you any good at apologising?

How do you react to apologies?

Crying Openly Or In Secret

What are your thoughts on crying in front of your children? How do they respond to you when you cry? How do they respond to other people when they cry? What about crying in general?

Many adults are uncomfortable with crying. We try and make it stop, either when its other people or ourselves. The subliminal message, or even the actual message, is that crying is not acceptable.

"People Who Cry Are Weak And It Is Messy"

Do you really think our creator gave us the ability to cry, including the tear ducts, for no reason at all? That is ridiculous. It is like saying OMG why have we got these legs, put them away and do not use them or show them to anyone. It must be a glitch in the matrix.

Healing - When my girls that I coach reach a break down and send me voice notes of them crying and in pain, it lets me know that they are doing the work and in a couple of days they will get rewarded. It is a sign of progress.

Expression – Crying is also a form of expression and communication. I feel sad, I cry, my face gets wet and I sound annoying. It passes. Next! Imagine if babies did not cry, how would we know they were hungry or too hot? Here are a few things crying shows our children:

- All people cry.
- It is a healthy release of sadness.
- We do not have to be uncomfortable being around someone who is crying.
- We do not have to be ashamed of our emotions.
- Crying is a sign of being human
- Crying is temporary.

This is at a healthy rate, if your crying is excessive and not bringing you space and healing, seek further support.

ww.consciousfamilydynamics.com

Yelling Trigger

What triggered your yelling?

How long have you been doing this?

What was the pattern?

How can you interrupt that next time?

Guilt Gift

What is the guilt trying to tell you?

What triggered my guilt?

What needs to be let go?

How can I interrupt that next time?

seasoned

PART: FOUND

"I Am The Process"

And What A Powerful
Process I Am.

"Life Is Orgasmic

surrender, receive, let go and then go again"

Welcome To Life!

Oh my goodness that was such a wonderful beautiful magical journey you guys. Thank you so much for coming with me on it. I hope you felt it, I hope you felt inspired, I hope so much that you got more than you ever could have imagined you could from it.

What have you learnt about yourself, about your process, about …life?

Who are you? Declare it to the world!

I am
_____
_____
_____
_____

Everybody processes things differently, yet we have fundamentals that are the same. What works for you may not work for the next person and vice versa.

The journey will never end because life is the journey. Where are you heading now? What are you creating with all this space? How much more can you expand to allow the universe to give to you?

Honestly, life is like an orgasm. There are tension orgasms and relaxed orgasms. Do you have to be in control to orgasm or can you relax and receive? Do you have multiple orgasms or multiple on multiple orgasms? Or none?

Life really is about the foreplay, the penetration, the relaxing, the orgasm and the cuddles afterwards. Remember, it is not just about the climax.

Make your life orgasmic!

As for me:

I chase freedom like a dog on heat chases a bitch. I sleep at night knowing that I have started a love affair with myself so deep no one will ever be able to destroy it. I look in the mirror seeing my true inner beauty. I have shed back the layers that kept me stuck small and have risen and risen and risen. I have a powerful tribe of soul sistas that in a heartbeat would march to my drum, just as I march to theirs. I have my crown. I have my heels. I have my sword. I slay. I twirl. I seek peace. I meditate. I am being more me than I ever have before.

When I laugh, its real. When I say no, I mean it. When I call myself kind, I know the definition of the word. When I say loyal, I don't mistake that for selfish. I will cry. I will cuss. I will run my mouth. I never stay down for long. I have become the woman I needed when I was falling apart. I have become my own inspiration.

I am the woman who is standing up. I am the woman who will always spit the truth. I am the woman who knows exactly what her intuition sounds like. I am the woman who seeks freedom at all costs. I am the woman who has turned this pain into empowerment. I am the woman who will lead other women to the same strength and fulfillment that I now feel. I am the woman who is showing people the way out of the dark and into the light. I am a way-shower. I am where my feet stand. I am power!

Keep an eye out for my workshops, books and coaching offers. I am always open to collaborations so if you have something we can vibe together on, holla at your homegurl!

I Am April And I Am Your Intuitive Parenting Coach And This Is A Dream Come True. I Am Published!

Upcoming Book Draft

Co-Operative Parenting Through Break Ups

This is the rising and returning of the parents.

Before we begin. This isn't going to be just a book of inspiration.

A book to take you through the emotional highs and lows of my life. Nope. Maybe the next book can be that? To be fair, I don't feel like I've had that many experiences. Mmmm let me see.

So, I've experienced Infertility. Miscarriage. Infidelity. Been on the verge of bankruptcy. Been physically abused and knocked out. Had someone I was very close to go to jail for manslaughter. Had people I've been close to addicted to methamphetamine. Had my marriage fall apart after 15 years of a relationship. Grown a business from the ground up. Gotten fat. Yeah so not too much really. Nothing significant.

What this is going to be is a book that shows you the lessons I learnt from my journey and it's going to be from my heart. No filtering to be 'publishable'. If the publisher doesn't like it, fuk them. Its raw. Its real.

It's Me Being Me In This World.

And last but not least, it's going to have calls to action. For you.

You aren't going to just read a book and take no action. That's so last week man. Its time. And as the legend himself Mr. Joel Brown says, it's all about the POP. Ok, no he doesn't say that. He says it's the power of practice. It's all good to just read, absorb and be the most knowledgeable person in the world.

But what the fuk is knowledge without experience? Unless you're a book yourself, nada babe, nada.

Get moving.

"Where There Is A Willingness, There Is A Way"

Learnings

What have you learnt?

Learnings
What have you learnt?

Celebrating You
What have you overcome and created?

Celebrating You
What have you overcome and created?

"You Must Fill Your Cup First"

These beautiful woodland photos throughout this book, were taken by **Acacia Lily Photography.** She is a Hamilton based mama and I instructed her to make sure she captures the emotion and connection. I didn't make it easy for her either because for me, a lot of that meant talking. I am so happy with these photos and they never get old.

"Books Tell Of Better Days"

There are so many books I recommend, from children's books to adults. Fiction and nonfiction. I won't make space to list them al here, but I will have them on my website.

"To thrive we need to feel safe. If we create a safe space for our children to learn the world, they will thrive. If you do not, they will live only to survive."

We Are Tangata Whenua | We Are The People Of The Land.

If I am truly from the land where my feet stand
then my tears are the salt
that oozes from our mother's eyes
she is sad
she is hurting
her children are in pain
her children are fighting

there is yet again mass blood
spilt over her body

she is asking us to stop
stop the fighting
stop the slandering
stop the judgement
stand together with all our differences
can't you see what is happening here
the boy with the egg
the parents
keyboard warriors
laughing
pointing
judging
condemning another to shame
because they spoke freely
Mama Earth is in so much pain
right now
and it is coursing through my body
out of my eyes
in my blood
is everyone this blind to what is happening here
here on our land
here in
Aotearoa

no, we are not a land of innocence anymore no we are not a mighty host
we have been brought to dishonour and shame
but not from 1 man's hate
but from our nations state
when will we wake
when will our people see
that to stand as one
we must accept we have lineage
we are from the land
peace, not war, shall be our boast
yet the war through technology
every minute
of every day
the tragedies
being heightened
by anger and hatred between our people
we are saying
we stand together
we are saying
we are one
but we are lying
to each other
yes, mother earth she is crying
she is doubled over in grief
this is not what our people fought for
we did not lose many an ancestor for this
we ask for a treaty
we ask for freedom of speech
we ask to keep our enemies away
yet
it appears
they already dwell here

"Not Today Satan, Not Today"

Big Aroha.

April B – Your Intuitive Parenting Coach

Insta: @iamaprilbroomhead

www.consciousfamilydynamics.com

Hamilton, New Zealand

www.ingramcontent.com/pod-product-compliance
Lightning Source LLC
Chambersburg PA
CBHW062021290426
44108CB00024B/2732